WOMEN
COUNT

[
A Guide to
Changing the World
]

SUSAN BULKELEY BUTLER
with **BOB KEEFE**

Purdue University Press

Published by
Purdue University Press
504 West State Street
West Lafayette, Indiana 47907
www.thepress.purdue.edu

Book Design by Anna Christian

Library of Congress Cataloging-in-Publication Data

Butler, Susan Bulkeley.
Women count : a guide to changing the world / by Susan Bulkeley Butler ; with
Bob Keefe.
    p. cm.
ISBN 978-1-55753-569-6
1. Women—Political activity. 2. Leadership in women. 3. Social action.
4. Social change. 5. Feminism. I. Keefe, Bob. II. Title.
HQ1236.B88 2010
305.420973'09045—dc22
                                        2010007998

Printed in the United States of America

To all who made an impact
on today's women,
and to everyone who will influence
permanent equality
for women around the world.

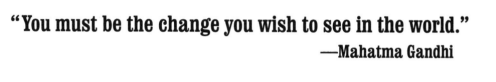

"You must be the change you wish to see in the world."
—Mahatma Gandhi

[CONTENTS]

[INTRODUCTION]

A NEW MOVEMENT

REGULARLY NOW, I see encouraging reports that the world is changing for the better for women. These are welcome signs along a journey that for me began over forty years ago.

The U.S. Department of Labor reports that women now make up almost 50 percent of the nation's workforce.

Fortune magazine states that the number of Fortune 500 women CEOs increased four-fold in the past decade (albeit to a mere fifteen in 2009).

Maria Shriver's "A Woman's Nation" report informs readers that 40 percent of mothers are now their family's primary breadwinner, and 60 percent of mothers bring home at least one-fourth of their family's income.

Time magazine reports that 54 percent of men and 69 percent of women say they believe there would be fewer problems in the world if there were more women in business and government.

For as long as I can remember, the world first ignored, then focused on counting women's accomplishments. Each time a barrier is broken, another marker is posted along the way.

I experienced this firsthand. In 1965, I became the first professional female employee at Arthur Andersen & Co. Fourteen years later, I was the first woman partner at Andersen Consulting, a division of Arthur Andersen & Co. that became Accenture, one of the world's largest management consulting, technology services, and outsourcing companies.

Make no doubt about it: The accomplishments of women in recent years are truly astounding and well worth celebrating. But tallying numbers is no longer enough. We've done that. It's no longer enough to count women—it's time to ensure that we are all women who count.

Women's history has been one change, one movement, after another. We earned the right to vote. We kept the country running while men fought World War I and World War II. We freed ourselves from our traditional roles. We entered the workplace, and we made our way through the pipeline of every conceivable profession.

Now we need to create change to ensure women are equal partners in making the world a better place for everyone, a place where all women count.

We need another movement.

I am no radical. I realize the word "movement" may scare some people. But it is necessary. The movement I am advocating now is simply about changing our thinking, putting what we already know about women into action, and making change that is not a temporary Band-Aid, but a permanent solution.

It's not surprising that *Time* magazine reported in October 2009 that most people think that having more women leaders would help solve the world's problems. Women, after all, tend to be more compassionate. They tend to take less competitive approaches to issues. And they are typically better listeners and consensus-builders. Yet women represent only a fraction of the world's leaders.

Numerous studies show that companies run by women significantly outperform their industry peers. Yet women still only make up about 3 percent of the CEOs of Fortune 500 companies.

Women know that to succeed they must depend on support from other women. Yet based on research, women are not actively mentoring, developing, and promoting other women within their organizations.

The timing is right for things to change. Finally, women have the numbers, the education, the track record, and the characteristics necessary to change the world, and the world needs the skills and the attributes of women more than ever.

Now is the time to leverage our numbers and our accomplishments as a collective body, to demonstrate our passion, and to make the world a better place—not just for women, not just for men, but for all.

It's time for you to join the new movement. Let's get going.

The
New
Math

1
By the Numbers

I'VE ALWAYS BEEN about numbers.

At Abingdon High School (Class of 1961) in Abingdon, Illinois, (population 3,500), math courses such as algebra and calculus were always my favorite subjects. I had little use for courses with lots of reading, but give me a problem, show me an equation, and I could solve just about anything.

When my family's company got its first computer punch card machine to help track orders and sales, I became enamored with its capabilities, even though my official summer job at our American Sanitary Manufacturing Co. (makers and purveyors of bathroom plumbing fixtures and stainless steel swimming pool equipment) was as the telephone operator.

Later, I went to work about ten miles away at the Maurita Dale dress shop in the "big city," Galesburg, Illinois (population 37,000). It was a great weekend job, helping Mrs. Manwarren, the shop owner. Like many high school girls, I loved seeing the new fashions and feeling the new fabrics, but what I liked even more was waiting on the customers, making the sales and tallying them up at the end of the day. And, of course, I liked getting the discounts on all of my purchases.

My role model for how to dress was one of my math teachers, Shirley Castle. She always dressed to the hilt: beautiful skirts and sweaters, high heels, and pearls. I am always reminded of her when I talk about the importance of one's "packaging." It is all about the image one leaves. The image Mrs. Castle left is very clear to me, even to this day.

I thought about being a mathematician.

Instead, I decided to get a business degree from Purdue University, with a minor in mathematics. It served me well. Fresh from college, I became the first woman professional hired at the Big Eight accounting firm, Arthur Andersen & Co., and would later become the first woman partner of the firm's consulting division, now known as Accenture. I eventually rose to the position of Managing Partner of Accenture's Office of the CEO before retiring in 2002. Now in my second career as the founder and CEO of the Susan Bulkeley Butler Institute for the Development of Women Leaders, through which I spend much of my time coaching and mentoring women, I find math, numbers, and my experience as a woman in business intersecting once again.

Women have made great strides since those times when many companies would not even let me interview for a job with them because I was a woman. Even Arthur Andersen had to make sure that its clients would accept "a man in a skirt." (By this I mean, that the only other people on the professional staff were men, hence the quote "man in a skirt.")

But even now, when women are more involved than ever before in the workplace, in government, and in their communities, I constantly hear it over and over again, both from the women I coach and mentor and from the little voice in my own head: *Do women count?*

The answer, of course, is yes. Women represent over half of the country's population, over half of the country's college graduates, and nearly half of the country's workforce. But look at the nation's corporate boards and executive level offices, look at top ranks of government and civic groups, industries like financial services and utilities, look anywhere except the stereotypical "women's" fields of teaching, nursing, and retailing, which haven't changed since my days at Mrs.

Manwarren's Maurita Dale dress shop. One will quickly realize that the percentage of women in those top roles aren't nearly reflective of society as a whole.

Do women count?

Of course they do, but not like they *should* in the roles that matter most in today's world. Consider some numbers:

- Less than 3 percent of the top executives in America's biggest companies are women.
- Less than 16 percent of the directors of Fortune 500 companies in America are women.
- Only 17 percent of members of Congress are women. As of early 2010, only six of the nation's fifty governors are women.
- Four decades after Congress passed the Equal Pay Act, women still earn an average of seventy-eight cents for every one dollar a man earns.

When pictures of executive teams are displayed, there may be only one woman. In technology companies, the women are typically in the marketing or human resources departments. That's because those are the expected roles for women. In financial services (e.g., banking, stock brokerages, etc.) there are few women at the decision tables.

Look in any history book and one will find that the vast majority of figures mentioned are men. How many kids grow up learning about Douglas MacArthur or Franklin Roosevelt? How many know about Deborah Sampson or Elizabeth Blackwell? (We'll get to them later . . .)

Few people are as knowledgeable about the underrepresentation of women in history as Molly Murphy MacGregor. In 1972, as a fresh new schoolteacher, she proposed teaching a semester-long women's history class at her school. A colleague quickly asserted that such a class really shouldn't take more than an hour, because women hadn't done that much throughout the course of history anyway. A few years later, MacGregor and some of her colleagues took an inventory of women in teacher-training textbooks. Their finding: Less than 3 percent of the content of the books mentioned the contributions of women. Contributions of women of color and women in fields such as math, science, and art were generally excluded, despite the accomplishments of luminaries such as Barbara Jordan, Georgia O'Keeffe, Wilma Rudolph, and Sojourner Truth. When women were included in the textbooks, MacGregor and her colleagues found the majority were mentioned only as footnotes.

Think about that for a minute.

Footnotes.

Yes, men fought our battles and explored our world and pioneered business and industry. But what were the women doing all that time? Didn't they do anything to help along the way? Didn't they accomplish or contribute anything worth more than a few *footnotes*?

The importance of recognizing women in history isn't just about getting credit where credit is due. When girls read history textbooks and see few mentions of women, what kind of aspiration does that give them to make history on their own? At the same time, when boys read those same textbooks and come to the realization, inaccurately or not, that it's their gender that has always led the world, led the country, led the companies, how is that going to affect their attitudes toward women? We are all products of our history. If women think their contributions to history are only a fraction of men's, it's going to continue to be hard for any woman to contribute more than just a fraction of her true and total potential.

Think about it this way. How many people have been inspired by Martin Luther King, Jr.? How many people would aspire to live his dream and attain his goals if his contributions weren't well-chronicled in history books, if he didn't have a day named after him, and if he wasn't memorialized around the world?

Here's another way to look at it. How many boys have wanted to be an astronaut because of what they've read about Neil Armstrong or John Glenn? How many young male scientists were inspired after learning about Albert Einstein or Louis Pasteur? What budding young businessman hasn't gotten some aspiration from what they've read or seen about Bill Gates, Henry Ford, or Andrew Carnegie?

Now think about what sort of influence it would have on science-minded girls if they were taught as much about the accomplishments of pioneering astronomer Maria Mitchell or astronaut Sally Ride as they were about Neil Armstrong or John Glenn? What would be the effect on girls who have a penchant for writing if Louisa May Alcott or Phillis Wheatley, the first African-American woman to publish a book, were as widely known as Robert Frost or Walt Whitman? How many more Hispanic women would be inspired to greatness if only they knew as much about the accomplishments of Dolores Huerta, co-founder of the United Farm Workers, as they knew about César Chávez, founder of the first successful farm workers' union?

In 1980, MacGregor set about to rectify the lack of recognition of women in history. She and others started an institution called the National Women's History Project. They successfully convinced President Jimmy Carter to designate the week of March 8, 1980 as the first National Women's History Week. Seven years later, they convinced Congress and Ronald Reagan to designate all of March as National Women's History Month. Recognition of women's contributions to history has certainly improved, but there's a long, long way to go. In history books, in the pages of today's newspapers and magazines, women are still under-recognized, underappreciated, and as a result, underrepresented as potential role models for girls and young women.

MacGregor and others at the national Women's History Project still realize they have much work to do. In considering the theme for their 2010 anniversary celebration, they decided on: "Writing Women Back into History." Thirty years later, the project's founders and many others still realize the numbers don't add up when it comes to women in history—past, present, and future. Like me, they are stuck contemplating that same nagging question: *Do women count?*

2
Changing the Equation

Why don't the numbers add up for women? Partly it has to do with basic discrimination that still exists today, despite the introduction of numerous laws over the years. Partly it's because there aren't enough women who strive to be CEOs and members of boards of directors, and not enough people are mentoring and supporting others to help women reach such heights. Partly it's because there just aren't that many of those sorts of positions available, due to lack of turnover.

Maybe the numbers we are counting are the wrong ones.

Women and their supporters have been lobbying for equal pay in the workplace since at least the 1800s. At its annual convention in 1868, the National Labor Union (a predecessor to the American Federation of Labor, the AFL in AFL-CIO) demanded equal pay for women, but it wasn't until fifty years later that states around the country, led by Montana and Michigan, began adopting equal pay laws. Another thirty years would pass before Congress would begin to consider national laws that mirrored what was happening at the state level. The Equal Pay Act of 1963 was supposed to ensure that women throughout the country receive the same pay as men for equal work. The Civil Rights Act of 1964 was supposed to prohibit employment discrimination based on race, sex, color, religion, or national origin.

Yet despite all of that, women are still typically paid less than their male counterparts; they still are denied promotions to senior levels because of their gender; they still are subjected to sexual harassment in the workplace, whether blatant or benign; and sexual discrimination complaints are still rising. In 2008, there were nearly 28,400 charges of sexual discrimination filed with the Equal Employment Opportunity Commission, up 16 percent from a decade earlier and the highest number on record. Despite all the laws, all the changes in public perception, all the sexual harassment training (or perhaps because of it), more women complain about discrimination than ever before.

Another reason the numbers don't add up for women is because of their historical role in society. In the early 1900s, a woman's place was truly in the home. Women were seldom seen in the workplace outside of family businesses or farms. By the 1960s, when I was in college and preparing to start working, women made up a third of the employed population, and the numbers were rising. Still, I and countless other women entering the workplace at that time had to convince our male job interviewers that we were capable of doing the same work as men. Companies that hired women for jobs outside the factory floor or the secretarial pool were few and far between. Today, of course, it's better. But how many times are women passed over for positions by men who think they just aren't ready for that job or haven't been prepared, at least in part because they are women?

In my first book, *Become the CEO of You, Inc.* (Purdue University Press, 2006), I laid out some of the lessons I learned along my career path to becoming the first female partner of Andersen Consulting, now Accenture. In order to be successful in business, I wrote, you have to pave your own path, make your own plan, and find mentors and teammates to help you along the way to your goals. You have to learn to ask for what you want. You have to make things happen *for* you—rather than let things happen *to* you.

But since that book was published, I've come to realize that for many women, success isn't necessarily limited to business success. Through contacts made through my book and my institute, I have met countless women who are successful leaders in their families, in their communities, in their homes. For many, success might not mean being CEO of a company; it might mean being a good CEO of your home. It might mean being a good role model for others, or a good member of your community.

I have also met successful mothers who gladly chose to give up their full-time jobs to homeschool their children; women who started amazing nonprofits to help improve their communities or their countries; philanthropists who put their money where their hearts are to improve the world; and mentors and coaches who devoted their time and their energy to helping others succeed. I am sure you know women who have done all these things. Maybe you are one of them yourself.

My thought in writing this book was that even though women may have different goals or ideas about success, we can all learn from our collective history and our common experiences as women to give us the tools to take us down that path to success, whatever success is to us individually.

A good friend of mine in Tucson is Zara Larsen, a former global automotive and aerospace/defense executive. She now is president of The Larsen Group: Architects of Change, a private consulting firm dedicated to helping others unleash their true potential by clear and transformational change. A big supporter of women's issues, Zara also hosts the "Circles of Change" radio show that delves into organization, career, and life change opportunities and issues. Zara is an unsung hero to many women who have heard a message from her radio show that changed their life.

A few years ago, I was privileged to be a guest on Zara's show to discuss my first book and career issues for women. One of the fundamental issues women face today, I said, is that most women tend to think of everybody else before they think of themselves. Maybe it has to do with maternal instinct, the traditional roles of women, or just the way we've been "programmed" to take care of others.

Either way, it hit a chord with many listeners.

"I do this all the time!" one woman commented after my appearance on Zara's show. "I feel selfish if I put myself before others. In jobs and in personal life, I bend over backward for employers and friends but don't go so far out of the way for myself."

As long as women continue to think about others before themselves, they will probably remain in the current category of "women who are counted" but will probably not be among the "women who count."

To become women who count, women need to change their own equations. That means stretching beyond their traditional roles and their traditional goals. That means not just thinking about how to help others, but how to help themselves. It means moving beyond positions of support and into positions of leadership. And it means creating a new vision of how you see yourself—and other women—in the world.

How? That depends on your idea of success.

For the woman in business, it may mean setting a goal to become CEO instead of being content as a vice president of marketing or sales. For the wife or mother, it might mean taking the time for your own ambitions—maybe starting that nonprofit you've always been thinking about, getting more involved in your community, even running for office instead of solely supporting your husband's ambitions and your family's needs. For the mother, it might mean taking a leadership role in the school PTA or perhaps even homeschooling your kids instead of just sending them off to school each day and complaining about what they aren't—and are—getting in their education.

Think of the results and the potential if women could and would take greater leadership roles in their businesses, their communities, our world. Think of how the financial debacle of 2008-2009 could have been different had there been more women in decision-making positions in financial services companies.

Just prior to the 2008 presidential election, award-winning *New York Times* columnist Nicholas Kristof compared the accomplishments of women and men leaders over history. Sure, there had never been a woman president in the United States, Kristof pointed out, but history gives us plenty of lessons of the successes of women leaders elsewhere: Cleopatra of Egypt, Catherine the Great of Russia, Wu Zetian of China, and Queen Elizabeth I of England, to name a few.

"I have to acknowledge it," Kristof wrote. "Their historical record puts men's to shame."

You don't have to be Cleopatra or Catherine the Great to count. But you do have to change your equation if you want to be more successful in your world.

Dee Dee Myers was press secretary for former President Bill Clinton. In her 2008 book *Why Women Should Rule the World* (Harper-Collins, 2008), Myers set out a great vision of what it might be like if women took more leadership roles in the world. Businesses would be more productive, Meyers surmises. Politics would be more collegial, and communities would be healthier. Why? Quite simply, because women are different from men. They tend to be better communicators, better listeners, and better consensus-builders.

The numbers bear out the potential impact of women leaders in business, at least. A 2007 study for Catalyst Inc., a nonprofit group focused on expanding opportunities for women in businesses and professions, found that companies with the most women on their boards of directors outperformed those with the least number of women directors by 53 percent or more when measured by return on equity. A separate study done for Catalyst found that companies with the highest representation of women in their top management teams experienced about a 35 percent higher return on equity and return to shareholders than companies with few or no women in the their top management.

History has given us countless women who have changed the world, whose lives have counted. And now more than ever, the future holds limitless opportunities for us all to make our lives count and our worlds better.

It's up to us to sum up the lessons of the past, add in the opportunities of the future, and change our equations, both collectively and individually, to pave our path to success—however we may view success.

3
A Better Formula

CLEARLY, THERE'S NEVER BEEN a better time for women to make history.

Yes, women are still at a disadvantage to men, and gender-based discrimination still exists. By some measures, things may be getting worse, not better. As U.S. Representative Carolyn Maloney recounted in her compellingly titled book *Rumors of Our Progress Have Been Greatly Exaggerated* (Rodale, 2008), a Government Accountability Office study she helped commission found that the wage gap between men and women managers in many industries actually *grew* between 1995 and 2000. Further, as Maloney writes, a U.S. Census Bureau report found that the percentage of women in executive management positions actually *fell* from 32 percent in 1990 to 19 percent in 2000.

So why do I optimistically say there's never been a better time for women to make history?

Turn back to the trends for a minute. More women are graduating with undergraduate and graduate degrees than ever before. Leadership opportunities in business, government, and in the community are growing every day. Men are more involved in their families than ever before, giving women more freedom to pursue their interests in work, public service, philanthropy, and other areas.

Perhaps most importantly, public thinking and public policy is finally catching up again when it comes to considering the rights and opportunities of women and the importance of their contributions.

Nothing illuminated this more than the 2008 presidential election.

More than thirty women have been nominated by political parties for president of the United States, beginning with women's suffrage leader Victoria Woodhull in 1872. If you don't recognize Woodhull's name, you probably won't recognize many of the other female candidates for president either, such as Linda Jenness, Lenora Fulani, or Marsha Feinland. Before 2008, they were some of the top vote-getters of any female presidential candidate in the United States. They also were the nominees of political parties you may have never heard of, such as the Socialist Workers Party (Jenness's party in 1972), the New Alliance Party (Fulani's party in 1988), and the Peace and Freedom Party (Feinland's party in 1996).

Geraldine Ferraro forever changed history in 1984 when she became the first female vice-presidential candidate to receive a major party's nomination, as Walter Mondale's running mate on the Democratic ticket.

But in 2008, everything changed again.

Hillary Clinton came closer than any other woman in history to securing a presidential nomination from a major party. In seeking the Democratic nomination, she won twenty-one states and more than eighteen million votes, beating Barack Obama in the popular vote but narrowly losing to him in the race for delegates. On the other side of the political aisle, vice presidential nominee Sarah Palin helped John McCain win more than fifty-seven million votes, about twenty-two million more than Ferraro won with Mondale nearly a quarter-century earlier. And though largely unnoticed, the most recognizable "third party" in the United States, The Green Party, also nominated a woman, former Georgia Congresswoman Cynthia McKinney, as its pick for president. McKinney, who also is an African-American, received only 161,000 votes, but still more than any other woman-led, third-party presidential candidate since Fulani ten years earlier.

While America didn't elect a woman president, the 2008 election and the support that Barack Obama got from women raised the awareness, the potential, and the opportunities for women to new highs. His actions in his first year in office reinforces my thinking that there has never been a better time for women to make their mark on history.

The first piece of legislation Obama ever signed was the Lilly Ledbetter Fair Pay Restoration Act, which guarantees equal pay for equal work, regardless of gender. A few weeks later, he created the White House Council on Women and Girls to make sure every major federal agency considers how their policies and programs affect women and families. Obama's cabinet and his senior staff include more women than any president before him. Women he appointed to his cabinet, such as Department of Homeland Security Secretary Janet Napolitano, Department of Health and Human Services Secretary Kathleen Sebelius, and of course Secretary of State Clinton almost assuredly will continue to make their mark on the advancement of women for decades to come. Obama's appointment of U.S. Supreme Court Justice Sonia Sotomayor put a woman on the highest court of the land. His pick for U.S. Surgeon General, Regina Benjamin, puts a female face on the most influential doctor's office in the country.

While all those women and all those policies are important, it is also important to remember the women behind the man. They represent another side of the influence women have on society, and their contributions deserve to be recognized in history books as well. They also represent the amazing potential and opportunity that all women have and show that one doesn't have to become a top business executive, a top political office holder, or a zillionaire philanthropist to make history.

Madelyn Payne was an ordinary woman from an ordinary place, who wanted little more than to live an ordinary life. Up until her final days, that's pretty much what she did. The daughter of an office clerk, Payne grew up in middle-class America, got married a few weeks before graduating high school, and went on to get a job at a bank, have a daughter, and help raise her daughter's son like grandmothers all across America have done for centuries.

Except for her name, Payne's daughter Stanley Ann Dunham was also a typical American girl, of another generation. But Ann, as she became known after eschewing the name given to her by her father who had hoped for a son instead of a daughter, went on to travel the world, become an anthropologist, weather two broken marriages, and raise two children.

One of those children was Barack Obama. In his memoirs and speeches, Obama points to his mother Ann Dunham and his grandmother Madelyn Payne—"Toot," as she was affectionately known in Hawaiian parlance—as the foundation of his life and the source and inspiration of his values. Imagine who Obama might have become if not for the inspiration of the two women who raised him after his father left the family to return to his African homeland. Imagine if those women weren't strong enough to raise a boy on their own (with help from Obama's grandfather, Stanley Dunham) or if they didn't teach him all they could about life and love and persistence and pain and everything else he learned in his formative years. Imagine how many single mothers and grandmothers are raising children today who will become our next presidents, our next leaders of industry, our next historical figures. (Obama, of course, wasn't the only successful president who credited his success to his mother. Another American president, George Washington, once uttered the immortal phrase: "All I am, I owe to my mother.")

There are a few other women who have influenced the forty-fourth president of the United States: His wife, Michelle, and daughters, Sasha and Malia. Tellingly, when pushing for new legislation on fair pay and establishing agencies like the White House Council on Women and Girls, Obama was quick to acknowledge that partially what drove him was the same thing that drives any father of girls: To make sure their daughters have the same rights and opportunities as anybody else.

There is something else that gives me reason to believe that equation is changing for women, something intertwined in the messages of hope, change, and new beginnings that got Obama elected. The election of 2008 was just an indication, in some ways, of the change that has washed over the rest of our world: Change in the way we work, the way we address our enemies and our economic challenges, the way we think about our families and our environment, and everything else that affects us.

The new world, I believe, is a world where the skills and experiences and strengths that women have—skills like dialogue and compassion; experiences like work and family integration and inclusion; strengths like spirituality and creativity—are more important than ever before.

It is all part of the new math, the changing equation that makes this a better time than ever for women to succeed. As you continue to read, hopefully you will discover the paths to take you on the journey toward success. Along the way, you have an opportunity to change the world.

But first, it's good to learn from the lessons of women who made history in the past: the women who changed our world in their own individual ways.

They are the pioneers, the catalysts, and the leaders.

4
Making It All Add Up

HISTORICALLY, THE PERCEPTION of success for men has meant advancing to the highest levels of business, politics, or sports.

That's it.

Not to diminish any man's success. Not everybody can be the company CEO, elected president, or win The Masters.

But for men, that's really about it.

Of course men have outside demands that in some cases can be just as difficult, or more difficult, than those placed on women. But when is the last time you heard about Phil Mickelson's fathering skills? How much time did a genius like Bill Gates really spend raising his children when he was building Microsoft? How many male corporate CEOs did you see at the last PTA or Girl Scout troop meeting?

The perception of success for women is different. To be a successful woman, you have to be a good employee, a good mother, a good lover, a good friend, not to mention a good sister/daughter/aunt/PTA member. Success for a woman encompasses much more than just success at work, regardless of occupation, status, or position. Women have to deal with a lot more than just climbing the professional ladder. Every facet of a woman's life must add up to achieve the public and personal perception of success.

Think about candidates for office. When former Alaska Governor Sarah Palin was campaigning for the White House with John McCain, one of the many controversies surrounding her candidacy involved her children and her role as a mother if she were to win office. The questions that ensued were no different than those that might face any other female candidate for any other job. Was she being selfish for pursuing such a lofty career instead of staying home and taking care of her children? Would she be able to raise her kids and do her job at the same time? Those same questions are asked behind the backs of almost any woman candidate for any major job. The only difference is that with Palin, they came front-and-center, on television talk shows, in newspapers, and at dinner parties and political gatherings.

Washington Post reporter Anne Kornblut details the double standard applied to female politicians in her 2009 book *Notes from the Cracked Ceiling* (Crown, 2009). In it, she describes how Palin and Hillary Clinton didn't lose the 2008 election because of their gender, but that their gender certainly didn't help them. Kornblut also details how other politicians have dealt with the potential political backlash of being a woman. Michigan Governor Jennifer Granholm, a former beauty queen, once used black-and-white pictures of herself during a campaign in an attempt to lessen her attractiveness, for instance. Others have taken similar steps to address the pitfalls of "hair, hemlines, and husbands" that are unique to being a female in politics.

Female athletes have their own set of unique issues that illustrate the differences between men, women, and success.

In 2006, tennis superstar Lindsay Davenport was near the top of her game. She began the year as the top-ranked female tennis player in the world. In February, she became just the eighth woman in history to win seven hundred singles matches. Later that year, Davenport reached the U.S. Open quarterfinals—just before announcing she was pregnant with her first child. After giving birth to son Jagger, Davenport struggled for two years to return to the prominence she once held, oftentimes with Jagger courtside near her. She never quite reached the level of play she once had. In 2009, faced with rising speculation she would retire, Davenport announced she would play in the Australian

Open. She had to withdraw soon after, though, after discovering they were having a child.

How many male athletes have had to put their careers on hold because they became pregnant? How many have had to try to return to the top of their game after putting their bodies through the physical challenge of childbirth?

Politicians and athletes are in the public eye, but every day, in every corner of the world, women face similar challenges as they juggle work, family, and life. Perhaps the biggest by-product of all that juggling is guilt.

Men face some feelings of guilt, too, when they're juggling work, family, and personal life, but I'd suggest not nearly as much so as women. That's because men know their role in the world well. It has been constant since the primal times of hunting and gathering. Men are born, raised, and bred to work, whether work means hunting for mastodons, raising crops on the farm, or clocking in at the office each day. They bring home the rewards of their work and the spoils of their conquests. They provide for their families. That's what men are programmed to do from their earliest days. How many times in their young lives are boys asked what they want to be when they grow up? How many times are they asked about how they want to raise their children?

Women once had a simple role as well. They were born and raised to take care of their families. Then that changed. Women were reprogrammed to help their husbands work the farms or fill in at the factories during wartime. Then they were reprogrammed again to stay home with their kids. Then they were pushed to go back to work. Then times changed again, and they were reprogrammed to pursue a career. Then, finally, they were reprogrammed to do all of it: go to work, help their spouse, and take care of their families.

Problem is, when one is juggling so many different duties and expectations, something is naturally going to get short shrift. And when that happens, something else is going to naturally arise: Feelings of guilt.

Guilt has become so prevalent among working mothers that a group of them even started a Web site (www.workingmomsagainstguilt

.com) and blog devoted to the topic. The group's credo explains it all: "We're moms. We work all day, bring home the bacon, and fry it up in a pan. Oh, and while we're at it, we're raising young children, along with our spouses/partners. As any working mom knows, we often battle the big 'G.' Guilt creeps upon us when we least expect it." Topics are indicative of the various struggles women everywhere deal with each and every day.

"As women, we're programmed from an early age with certain ideas of what 'good mothers' are like," blogger Susan wrote recently. "Most of us are taught that good mothers want to be with their children all the time, and have no other priorities in life but their children. We're told that work is sometimes a necessary evil, but we should want to stay home and dedicate our lives to kids (even if we can't afford to). After 20+ years of that programming, when we actually become mothers, reality clashes with our preconceived ideas of motherhood."

Writes another blogger named Sara: "When I had my first daughter, I worked in a 9-5 office and sent her to day care after six weeks. Guilt. My job also entailed a lot of travel. More guilt, especially because I got to stay in nice hotels and eat at fancy restaurants and pretty much enjoy time off from being a mom."

It's hard to be happy, and therefore hard to be successful, if one is feeling guilty. To be successful, then, women have to learn how to balance it all, to have it all—work, life, love, families, ambitions, everything adds up.

Perhaps nobody has figured this out better than my friend Barrett Avigdor, whom I know from my days at Accenture. She has been a lawyer for more than twenty-two years and a working mother for eighteen of those years.

"My work and my family are the most important parts of my life," Barrett told me. "For many years, I struggled with what felt like an impossible balancing act; trying to raise two sons and build a career at the same time."

On the surface, Barrett had it all. "I had a good career, my husband had a good job, we had a nice house in a fashionable suburb, two beautiful healthy boys, and the perfect nanny.

"Despite having it all, I was very unhappy," Barrett says. "My life was out of alignment with my values. I wanted to work full-time, but I wanted to raise my sons too. For a long time, I could not figure out what was wrong with me."

It turns out the only thing that was wrong was Barrett's approach to solving the complicated equation of her life. She was using an old formula for work and family life that just didn't fit her situation. As a result, she couldn't make it add up to happiness.

So Barrett made a change. After some long conversations with her husband and her leadership team at Accenture, she decided to redefine her position as a lawyer in the company's Chicago office. Her family moved to Tucson, where her parents lived. She began working from home. When she had to travel, her parents helped out with their grandchildren. It turned out to be a win-win situation for all.

"It was a big and very unorthodox move at the time, but it was the best thing I've ever done," she explained. "I know that what I did would not be right for everyone. But my message is that women need to decide what they really want and then go make that happen."

How happy is Barrett these days? So much so that she has written a book about it, literally. Barrett and co-author Cathy Greenberg's book *What Happy Working Mothers Know* (Wiley, 2009) is a must-read for any woman who wants to figure out how to make work and family life add up to success and happiness.

Figuring out how to make it all add up is becoming increasingly important—not just to women, but to the companies and organizations they work for. According to U.S. Census figures, about 40 percent of mothers with children over one year old were working in 1976. In 2006, about 70 percent of mothers with children over one year old were in the workplace. Every woman you see on the job who has a child also has all the myriad duties of a mother waiting for her when she leaves work. She also probably has a husband or partner to keep happy, a family to keep together, and a personal life to lead.

In December 2007, the London School of Economics released a study that found that working women toil for an extra 120 hours per year just to meet the unique demands of work and family that men don't usually have to worry about. Researcher Patrick McGovern discovered in interviews what every working mother already knows. Even when they're at work, working mothers have to keep their families running. Even when they leave the office, their job doesn't end. Women in more cases than not are responsible, or at least feel (or act more) responsible, for cooking dinner, cleaning, and making sure the kids get their homework done and get their clothes ready for school.

To be sure, men contribute more today than they ever have when it comes to caring for families and home life. But as McGovern's and other studies have found time and time again, women continue to be stretched and stressed much more than men as they strive for success.

"The pressures at work have been ramped up over the last 15 years, and the effect on women is striking," McGovern said in a story in London's *Daily Telegraph*. "If you are in a highly pressured job and have a fixed childcare arrangement, you may have to leave work at 5 p.m.—yet you are under the same (work) pressure as a man who can leave at 6:30 p.m."

McGovern's study also found that women's relationships with their children, their spouses, and other family members also are more adversely affected than men's because of added and increased work pressures.

It's not just working mothers who struggle with making it all add up. Women who have made the decision to put their families before their jobs also often struggle with balancing home life with personal life and their former or future careers.

My friend Tamara Keefe was a schoolteacher, then a professional corporate trainer for many years. After the birth of her first daughter, however, her outlook on life changed forever.

"I loved my job and was doing very well, but every time I went to work I couldn't help but think what I was missing out on: Those first smiles, those first words," Tamara explained. "When I actually was out of town on the day Delaney took her first steps, I realized I didn't want to miss anything else, ever again."

So instead of working full-time, Tamara began to work part-time for her same employer. After another daughter came along, then another, she began doing even less travel-intensive corporate train-ing work. Instead, she began studying and working on becoming a professional life coach, which essentially lets her do personal training and development work at home by telephone instead of by traveling out of town. She ultimately started her own nonprofit, called Live Love Now, that encourages people to approach everything they do out of love.

Tamara could care less about being a corporate CEO or being a world-class champion athlete. She was willing to give up income for more time with her family. For her, what adds up to success is a strong family and making a difference in people's lives. Like Barrett and like other successful women, Tamara has found her own unique way to make it all add up.

To move from being counted to counting, every woman has to figure out her own way to make all the disparate pieces of her life add up to success and happiness.

How do you do that?

In the next section, we'll learn the lessons of successful women who made history and changed the world by making it all add up for themselves. In the sections that follow, I'll propose some steps women can take to become "women who count."

The Pioneers

5
Leading Ladies

HER NAME WAS Deborah Sampson, but she was known as Robert.

Tall, lean, and muscular, Sampson could easily pass for a man, which is exactly what she did. Signing her enlistment papers as Robert Shurtlieff, she became the first American woman to ever join the Army.

Sampson came from humble beginnings, a direct descendent of Mayflower settlers. She grew up poor and struggling in colonial Plympton, Massachusetts. When she was five, her family got word that her father had drowned in a shipwreck, and her distraught mother split up the family in an effort to ensure her sons and daughters would lead better lives. Years later, the family would discover that Sampson's father was not dead, but had simply abandoned his family, found a new wife, and started a new family in Maine.

Even if her father wasn't, Deborah Sampson was principled. She grew strong by working on the farm of a church deacon with whom she was sent to live. On the farm, reading was discouraged, especially for women, but Sampson nonetheless taught herself to read from books she found, and tagged along to school whenever she could with the male children who also lived on the farm. Girls back then weren't supposed to go to school, after all.

Equipped with her newfound education and reading skills, she became absorbed in politics and the Revolutionary War by the time she was in her teens. Hearing and reading about the struggles and successes of the Continental Army and the promise of independence, her patriotism drove her to bind her breasts, impersonate a man, and enlist in the 4th Massachusetts Regiment. Her secret would remain with her for years. Once, in a battle in New York, she was hit by two musket balls in her thigh. Another bullet nearly split her forehead. Yet fearing discovery by a doctor, she snuck out of a field hospital and treated herself, digging out one of the musket balls with her own knife and closing up the wound with a standard sewing needle. Sampson— or Robert Shurtlieff, at least—was honorably discharged from the Army in October 1783.

Despite her bravery and her service, the new United States of America, where, as the Declaration of Independence had declared, "all men are created equal," turned its back on Sampson when the Army finally realized that she wasn't a he. Penniless and wounded by the war, she petitioned for back pay that the Army owed her but was declined because of the discovery of her gender. Though other members of the Continental Army received a pension for their service, she didn't. Throughout the years that followed, she borrowed money to survive from former soldiers who had served with her as well as from friends such as Paul Revere. It wasn't until decades after her discharge from the Army that Congress finally agreed to give her a portion of the pension she was owed for her service, marking the first step toward the eventual inclusion of women in the military.

History is filled with stories of women like Sampson, who overcame sexism and other odds to go on to greatness, even if their accomplishments went unrecognized and unappreciated. When I first started planning a book on how women can change the world in the future, I found myself constantly drawn to the past and the women who overcame the obstacles of their day to change their world, eventually for the better of all of us. We know many of them. But I found myself wanting to make sure that others who made history weren't forgotten by the history books. Their lives, I think, can be inspiration for us all and their lessons an integral part of any guide to making our own history.

Humble beginnings have often led to greatness.

In China there was Tz'u-hsi, a concubine to Emperor Hsien-feng, who for years was summoned and left naked at the foot of his bed at his whim before she won his favor by bearing him a son. In 1861, she and her son would succeed the emperor and she would go on to become one of the most powerful women in the world. Later known as the Dragon Lady or the Dowager Empress, Tz'u-hsi would bring China into the modern age, supporting the cause of poor Chinese in the Boxer Rebellion, outlawing inhumane practices like foot binding, allowing girls to go to state schools for the first time, and ending the prohibition of marriage between Chinese and Manchu residents.

Before Tz'u-hsi there was Theodora, the daughter of circus performers and a one-time actress who with husband Justinian became the ruler of the Byzantine Empire in the 500s. Since she was just a commoner, Justinian had to change Byzantine law just so he could marry Theodora, but they would ultimately rule together in the most powerful government of its time. While Justinian was regarded for his expansion of the empire through war and conquests, Theodora was known for advancing domestic policies. She may have been one of the world's first feminists and defenders of women's rights. Among other things, she liberated divorce, outlawed prostitution in some cities, and changed inheritance laws so women could benefit.

Theodora was the Princess Diana of her time, the most important and influential and best-known woman in the history of the Byzantine Empire. Other women who partnered with famous men changed history in less grandiose ways, sometimes with almost no recognition whatsoever.

In the early United States, there were women like Sampson but also others like Catherine Littlefield Greene, who invented the cotton gin. Greene was the mistress on a Georgia cotton plantation where she would watch slaves and other workers spend countless hours separating the seeds and other chaff from cotton. She began formulating the ideas for a machine that would help do the meticulous work for them. Since it wasn't considered proper at the time for women to hold patents, she passed her idea along to an aspiring young inventor named Eli Whitney. She supported him financially and otherwise for six months until he received a patent for the cotton gin in his name in 1793. Whitney went on to become recognized as one of the nation's greatest inventors; Greene faded away into obscurity.

Other women pioneers are better known, like the first American woman to appear on a circulating coin in the United States.

Susan B. Anthony was born to be a crusader. Her father Daniel was a Quaker and an abolitionist and her mother Lucy was a progressive who was active in the pursuit of women's rights when Anthony was growing up. Her parents took young Susan out of school and began homeschooling her after a teacher in New York refused to teach her long division because she was a female. Learning division, it seems, wasn't seen as necessary to a woman's life. Anthony went on, of course, to start with Elizabeth Cady Stanton the National Woman's Suffrage Association that eventually earned the right for women to vote in America. Along the way, Anthony was also a crusader for a wide variety of social issues, often taking personal risks and enduring constant criticism and scrutiny.

One of my prized possessions is a letter from Susan B. Anthony written to a distant relative, Colonel E. N. O. Clough that is dated December 15, 1863. In the middle of the Civil War, Anthony was working on one of her many petition drives, this one not for women's rights but for slave's rights. You can almost feel the drive, the passion, the cannot-fail attitude that personified her life in the words she wrote on the weathered page:

"We have near fifty thousand names already and hundreds of thousands are coming in daily, so that our hope for the million brightens," Anthony wrote. "If our first installment presented on the 14th Jan. shall number one hundred thousand, we shall have reached one tenth our million. At the present counting New York stands ahead—Penn. next. Kansas has sent in but two or three small lists. This can only be from the feeling of confidence—perhaps over confidence that slavery is killed dead, dead.

"But we must remember that changing the form of slavery does not remove the law of slavery. Our work is to compel the change of the law of the Nation. Until this work is actually done, the decree actually written and enforced, we shall not, cannot have peace. So long as slavery has a ghost of a hope of life it will struggle for a place."

What has always impressed me about Anthony, like Sampson and other women before her, is that she never let anything stop her. She set her goals, without regard to how lofty or unlikely, and then figured out ways to accomplish them. In 1836, nearly three decades before the Civil War, Anthony was already collecting petitions opposing slavery, even though there were laws at the time prohibiting such rabble-rousing. In the 1850s, she and Stanton started the first women's state temperance society, despite threats and ostracizing by men. Anthony and Stanton would also start the American Equal Rights Association, as well as a newspaper, *The Revolution*, that advocated equal rights for women and newly freed African-Americans. In 1872, Anthony was arrested for voting illegally in the presidential election. Despite a lifetime of struggling, protesting, and marching, it wasn't until fourteen years after Anthony's death that Congress finally added the 19th Amendment to the U.S. Constitution, giving women the right to vote.

About the time Anthony, Stanton, and others were organizing the women's suffrage movement, Elizabeth Blackwell was doing about the only job considered befitting of a woman in America of that time. She was a schoolteacher in Kentucky. Blackwell wanted more, however, even if it wasn't the norm. She made her mind up to achieve her goal. In 1847, the English immigrant began applying to medical schools across the country, something that was unheard of for women at that time. Only one, Geneva College in New York, accepted her, in part because administrators, faculty, and students thought her application was a hoax. It wasn't. Upon realizing this, the school, its faculty, students, and the entire town of Geneva rebelled against rebel Blackwell. She was allowed in but was ostracized from the beginning, forced to sit in the back of the classroom, shunned when she dared to ask questions, required to prove herself much more than any of her male classmates.

Despite the trials, on January 11, 1849, Blackwell graduated first
in her class, becoming America's first female doctor. Her challenges
were far from over, however. When she tried to practice medicine at
New York hospitals, she was turned away because of her gender. She
tried to open a private practice, but no landlord would rent space to
a female doctor. She finally bought her own home and started her
practice, seeing women and children there and making house calls
when her patients couldn't come to her. In the 1850s, she ended up
doing what no man would do: opening a dispensary in the slums of
New York City. Two other female doctors would join her, including
her sister Emily, who had followed in her famous sister's footsteps.
Together they would expand and incorporate Blackwell's dispensary,
creating the New York Infirmary for Women and Children. Not long
after, what had started as Blackwell's quest to become a doctor would
come full circle. In 1868, about twenty years after she had become the
nation's first female doctor, Blackwell opened the Women's Medical
College as part of her infirmary.

Eight hundred miles away in Chicago, Myra Bradwell was pioneering women's entry into another field. Like Blackwell, Bradwell
got her start as a schoolteacher but soon realized she had bigger
goals, and went for them. Being the wife of a lawyer-turned-state-
legislator, Bradwell was more knowledgeable about law than many
men. In 1868, she started the *Chicago Legal News*, which quickly
became the most widely circulated legal newspaper in the country.
The next year she took another major step. In August 1869, she took
and passed the Illinois Bar exam, accomplishing what she expected
would be the final step to becoming America's first female attorney.
The Illinois Bar had a different idea, however. Claiming in part that a
woman lawyer would be way too delicate to deal with brutal criminal
cases, the Illinois Bar refused to admit her. Accompanied by a male
attorney, Bradwell fought the decision all the way up to the U.S. Supreme Court. She lost all along the way. A relatively new member of
the Supreme Court, Justice Joseph Bradley, captured the sentiment
of the time in writing in his opinion from the bench in the case of
Bradwell vs. Illinois in 1872:

"The civil law, as well as nature itself, has always recognized a wide difference in the respective spheres and destinies of man and woman. Man is, or should be, woman's protector and defender. The natural and proper timidity and delicacy which belongs to the female sex evidently unfits it for many of the occupations of civil life. The constitution of the family organization, which is founded in the divine ordinance, as well as in the nature of things, indicates the domestic sphere as that which properly belongs to the domain and functions of womanhood. The harmony, not to say the identity, of interests and views which belong, or should belong, to the family institution is repugnant to the idea for a woman adopting a distinct and independent career from that of her husband . . . "

Times, however, were changing. It would take another twenty years, but Bradwell was finally admitted to the Illinois Bar. In 1892, she was admitted and approved to practice before the U.S. Supreme Court, the very body that had denied her the right to pursue her chosen career.

While women were fighting just to break into the workplace in America in the late 1800s and early 1900s, elsewhere they were breaking ground in other ways. In 1905, Austrian novelist and pacifist Bertha von Suttner became the first woman to become a Nobel laureate, winning the Nobel Peace Prize for her pacifist writings and work.

One of my personal heroes is Amelia Earhart. The girl from Kansas who broke so many barriers is known for becoming the first woman to fly solo across the Atlantic and for her mysterious disappearance during her 1937 attempt to fly around the globe. But her inspiring work with women was impressive as well. In 1935, Earhart joined the Department of Aeronautics at my alma mater, Purdue University, as a visiting professor and immediately began holding classes and sessions with women to teach them about the joys of flying and encourage them to pursue careers in aviation, or in whatever occupation their hearts desired. (Incidentally, Earhart's life has been chronicled in many ways, including the 2009 movie "Amelia" starring Hilary Swank, but the world's largest collection of her life's memorabilia is at Purdue.

Among other items in the collection is a White House admittance card for Earhart to visit another pioneer, first lady Eleanor Roosevelt, in December 1936—six months before Earhart's ill-fated attempt to circumnavigate the globe.)

"Someday," Earhart told women students at Purdue in 1935, "people will be judged by their individual aptitude to do a thing and (society) will stop blocking off certain things as suitable to men and suitable to women." Nearly fifty years later, Sally Ride would break another barrier and soar into another area once seen as unsuitable for women, becoming the first American woman in space when she blasted off from Florida aboard the space shuttle *Challenger.*

Earhart would also help start the "Ninety-Nines," a group for women pilots whose name was derived from its charter membership of ninety-nine licensed pilots of the day. Imagine, a woman's networking group in the 1930s! Earhart was its first president. Today, the organization that started with fewer than one hundred female pilots has more than five thousand members in thirty countries who provide scholarships and networking opportunities for female pilots and promote world fellowship through flight. How many women pilots have been inspired to fly by Earhart? It's impossible to count, but the path she set for the advancement of women in her chosen field is just as significant and just as notable as her flying feats. It's a model for mentoring for women in all walks of life.

For every Amelia Earhart, whose life has been chronicled, whose history has been preserved, whose tale has been told, there are thousands of women who also made history, but who were generally forgotten with time.

Ever heard of Valentina Tereshkova? Twenty years before Sally Ride became America's first astronaut, Tereshkova became the very first woman in space, when she blasted off from Russia aboard the *Vostok 6* rocket for a three-day mission orbiting the Earth to do experiments on the effects of space on females. Born in the same year of Amelia Earhart's fateful 1937 flight, Tereshkova was a textile worker before she was selected from more than four hundred candidates to become Russia's first cosmonaut in 1962.

You may know the name Bill Gates, but what about Grace Hopper?

Hopper defied the odds and joined the U.S. Navy during World War II, rising to the rank of rear admiral. Yet if her military service wasn't a big enough contribution, Hopper's mathematic prowess helped change and improve life for everyone. She used her math skills to help invent COBOL, one of the first and most revolutionary computer languages. Her software was used for complex ordinance calculations, done through one of the world's first large-scale digital computers, which she also helped invent, and would later become the foundation for the computer processing software we use every day.

Pioneers defied sexism and other odds to help shape countries and pursue their beliefs. Inventors changed the world, even if they didn't receive recognition. Daredevils and risk-takers paved the way for the future. Revolutionaries never gave up on their dreams, even if their dreams weren't reached until after their deaths.

To make our own history, to change our own world, we cannot sit still and float through life in the wake of the women who came before us. We must all be pioneers, inventors, risk-takers, and revolutionaries.

In the words of nineteenth century writer and *Little Women* author Louisa May Alcott, "It is as much a right and duty for women to do something with their lives as for men."

There's another quote often attributed to Alcott, a fitting one as we prepare to set about our own personal journeys on the way to making our own history and changing the world: "I'm not afraid of storms, for I'm learning how to sail my ship."

6
The Movement(s)

For every Amelia Earhart, every Susan B. Anthony, every Sally Ride, there have been countless other Amelias and Susans and Sallys who quietly, subtly, and probably unknowingly powered the wave of change for women that has brought us to this point where we can change the world once again.

The women I'm thinking about were those who ventured out into the workplace in the 1800s without fanfare or recognition. They are the women behind the men who watched the children, kept the home front running, and performed their social duties as their husbands climbed the rungs of politics and business to shape the country. They were the "farmerettes" of World War I; the "Rosie the Riveters" of World War II; the countless military wives who have had to raise children alone while their husbands were off in Korea or Vietnam or Iraq or Afghanistan. You won't find their names in history books. But without their collective sacrifices, we would be nowhere.

In America, the movement began in the New England factories of the early 1800s. Businessmen like Francis Cabot Lowell discovered he could hire young women and children much more cheaply than men and began recruiting them into the workforce. To assuage fears and counter complaints of worried parents, Lowell and others built boarding houses for the unmarried women and enforced strict disciplinary rules. From those factories, Americans learned that women could actually work outside the home, and that their families and American businesses could profit from their labor.

Other opportunities began to open for women as well. During America's Colonial Era, sending girls to school was often frowned upon as unnecessary, since a woman's place was caring for the children and running a household, not a business. By the 1800s, however, some schools had opened for women to teach them how to do the only job women of that time were seen fit for: Teaching. In New England, groundbreakers such as Sarah Pierce, Catharine Beecher, Zilpah Baniser, and Mary Lyon began a movement to create academies and seminaries to teach women how to teach. In 1832, Lyon helped create what today is Wheaton College and five years later would help start Mount Holyoke College, which would later become the model for other women's universities around the country.

Encouraged by what was happening in the Northeast, other parts of the country started exploring the possibilities of higher education for women. Ohio started the Oberlin Collegiate Institute in 1833, becoming the first school of higher education to admit both men and women. Two decades later, another co-ed school, Antioch College, also opened in Ohio. Across the Midwest and West, in places like Indiana, Utah, Kansas, and Nebraska, state-chartered schools began admitting women as well, teaching them more than just how to be teachers.

In 1884, Virginia Alice Cottey founded Cottey College in Missouri. When she was a child, Cottey had read a book about Mount Holyoke founder Mary Lyon, and from that day on, she was inspired to devote her time and energy to the education of women. Like Lyon, Cottey was a woman with a vision that women deserved the same education as men. In 1927, she gave her namesake college to the P. E. O. (Philanthropic Educational Organization) Sisterhood, whose mission is to promote educational opportunities for women. As a result, Cottey College is now the only non-sectarian U.S. college owned and supported by women, for women.

Women weren't the only ones concerned with furthering female education. In 1899, Simmons College was founded in Boston with a bequest from the estate of clothing manufacturer John Simmons. Simmons, whose industry had benefited so much from the work of women, wanted to create a university that could educate women "in useful professions" and help them find a path to live on their own, independent from men. It was a radical idea at the time. Seventy-four years later, Anne Jardim and Margaret Hennig would start Simmons' pioneering Graduate School of Management to provide graduate business education exclusively to women. The two also co-authored what is considered the seminal book *The Managerial Woman* (Anchor Press/Doubleday, 1977), which would become a bible for me and so many other executive women.

In 1870, The University of Michigan became the first major university to begin admitting women, paving the way for other universities to eventually do the same. One of the first women to attend Michigan was Alice Freeman Palmer. The daughter of a farmer-turned-physician, she desperately wanted to get a college degree from a leading university. In 1872, she took the entrance exam to Michigan, barely passed, and was admitted "under condition." Once in college, however, Palmer excelled. She became involved with many campus groups and was one of four speakers at her commencement in 1876. At Michigan, Palmer learned to be a teacher. She would go on to be one of the nation's greatest advocates for expanding education opportunities for women. In 1881, she became president of Wellesley College, and in 1892, she would become dean of the women's department at the University of Chicago. Throughout her lifetime, Palmer espoused the idea that women should further their education and become leaders, not followers, in both academia and life. In an 1898 speech entitled "Why Go to College?" she summed up the changing role of women in society at the turn of the twentieth century: "Our American girls themselves are becoming aware that they need the stimulus, the discipline, the knowledge, the interests of the college in addition to the school, if they are to prepare themselves for the most serviceable lives."

The 1800s also ushered in the beginnings of legal equity—if not equality—for women. Throughout the land, wives were still considered subservient to their husbands and legally were considered only a few rungs above property. If a husband and wife divorced (a rarity at the time), husbands retained the legal control of property and children in most cases. Change began in Mississippi in 1839, when the state passed laws to let married women own property on their own, separate from their husbands. Other states would follow.

Society was changing for women in other ways in the late 1800s and early 1900s. Even before they earned the right to vote, women were beginning to break political ground.

Before the world would ever know of Geraldine Ferraro or Hillary Clinton or Nancy Pelosi, there was Jeanette Rankin of Montana, who in 1917 became the first female member of Congress. Though she only served a single term in the U.S. House of Representatives, Rankin exemplified some of the attributes that a woman brings to political office that can help balance out some of the bravado of men, whether at the turn of the twentieth century or the turn of the twenty-first century. Rankin's first vote in Congress was against the U.S. entry into World War I. A suffragist, she would help push what then was called the Susan B. Anthony Amendment, which in 1920 became the 19th Amendment. While in office and after, Rankin would push for world peace, consumer rights, and child welfare through her support and involvement in groups such as the Women's International League for Peace and Freedom, the National Consumers' League, and the American Civil Liberties Union.

Rankin would usher in a new age for women in politics. On the heels of the 1920s passage of the 19th Amendment, Rebecca Felton of Georgia became the first woman to be elected to the U.S. Senate, in 1922. Oklahoma's Alice Robertson became the first female to preside over the U.S. House (for part of one day) that same year, and in 1923, Representative Mae Ella Nolan of California became the first female chair of a congressional committee. In the states, meanwhile, women also were making political inroads. In 1925, Nellie Tayloe Ross succeeded her late husband in Wyoming to become the first governor of a U.S. state. That same year, Miriam "Ma" Ferguson became governor of Texas, succeeding her husband James "Pa" Ferguson after he was impeached for a laundry list of improprieties.

In a speech shortly after her election, Ross described the sentiment of the time. Unfortunately, it sounds similar to the experiences of women who run for office to this day, including Hillary Clinton and Sarah Palin in their 2008 campaigns for the White House:

"It had created some excitement in Wyoming when a woman's bonnet was thrown (into) the contest for the office of governor," Ross said in prepared remarks preserved at the University of Wyoming. "There were those who exclaimed with amazement that a mere woman should have the temerity to offer herself for so important a position. Leaders of the opposing party sent emissaries to try by subtle methods to dissuade me, and at once they launched the slogan that 'A governor's office was no place for a woman.'

"Then when the election was over, establishing the victory of a woman, speculation was rife in many places as to what might happen in the executive offices of Wyoming," Ross said. "There were those who predicted that it would be the scene of many a pink tea. Others feared on the other hand some spectacular or revolutionary action there—perhaps a militant feminist program launched. The fear was voiced in some distant place that a woman governor might allow her heart rather than her head to control her and open the prison gates and set the worst criminals free. The records of Wyoming will in the future serve to refute such an argument used against any women in our own or other states who may offer themselves for the executive office."

While women were making inroads in politics, in society, and in the workplace, it would take war to begin the next great step in the early women's movement.

When the United States entered World War I in 1917, the country's Army and National Guard totaled about 200,000 volunteers—not nearly enough to fight overseas and defend the home front. To build ranks, in May 1917 Congress passed the Selective Service Act, drafting hundreds of thousands of men out of their jobs and their careers and turning them into doughboys to fight in the Great War.

The vacuum left the labor pool in America empty, and women stepped in to fill the job vacancies. Females who up until then were seen as the "leisure class," who barely had the right to vote, and barely had the right to higher education suddenly were a major part of the nation's industrial complex. Influential supporters of women's rights saw World War I as a call to action and an opportunity. In 1918, Harriot Stanton Blatch—the daughter of suffrage pioneer Elizabeth Cady Stanton—wrote her first book, *Mobilizing Woman-Power* (The Woman's Press, 1918) in which she recounted the rise of women during wartime and called for more women to seize the opportunities left behind by men who went to war to make more inroads in society.

"When men go a-warring, women go to work," Blatch wrote.

And during World War I, they did. Women for the first time found themselves working in the factories and on the railroad lines. They became messengers and elevator operators and took other positions that were considered taboo for women of the time.

In *Fruits of Victory* (Potomac Books, 2008), author Elaine Weiss recounts one of the more interesting and unheralded chapters in the women's movement during World War I. Farming was still the biggest part of the U.S. economy back then, and one of the biggest wartime concerns was over the availability of food, Weiss explains. President Woodrow Wilson went as far as to suggest that the country that was able to feed itself would win the war. With tens of thousands of farmers and farmhands leaving the land for the war overseas, it was up to women to fill the void. Following in the footsteps of British women, American women organized the "Woman's Land Army" to train thousands of housewives, city secretaries, teachers, and artists how to work the land. The "farmerettes," as they were known, donned uniforms and picked up shovels and hoes and spread out across the land from Florida to California to plant fields, bring in crops, and keep America fed. Without them, the country would have faced even greater shortages of food supplies than it did.

The "farmerettes," like all the other women who took up the running of the country during World War I, didn't do so without facing discrimination and sexism. Some farmers refused to hire women until they had no other choice. Other women kept a watchful eye on them, fearful that the city girls would try to steal their countrified husbands. Still others accused them of trying to take men's jobs, even though there were no men to fill them at the time. In *Fruits of Victory*, Weiss recounts a letter written by John Densmore, an official in the government Employment Service Office, to a leader of the Woman's Land Army as the group was winding down after the end of the war.

"The work done by the Woman's Land Army has not only been valuable in increasing the food supply when that was one of the most important questions before this country, but it has also demonstrated that women are able to do almost any kind of agricultural work and are specially fitted for certain branches of it," Densmore wrote. "I therefore feel that your work has not only helped us in our need but has added to our knowledge and has opened a new means of livelihood for women."

Densmore's letter may have given some pride and encouragement to the women who kept the nation's farms going, but with the end of the war, the status quo returned. Men returned home to take up their old jobs. The women who had filled them temporarily went back to their roles as housewives, society women, and clerical workers, the roles they had occupied in the years before the war and would continue to occupy for years after.

Women would stay in their roles as homemakers and wives until World War II. Then, just as Harriot Stanton Blatch had predicted in 1918, they would go back to work when men once again went "a-warring." This time, though, they would go back in even greater numbers and with greater consequences than ever.

Before the United States entered World War II, only about one in four women worked outside the home. Most were in secretarial jobs or similar occupations that held few opportunities for advancement. But just like World War I, the escalation of World War II pulled American men out of their jobs to go fight. At the same time, the government's unprecedented ramp-up of industry and the need for planes, tanks, and other war supplies created one of the greatest needs for workers the United States had ever seen.

Women once again filled in for the absent men, but this time they got more support than ever from the government and needy employers. Just as Uncle Sam was recruiting men to fight, he was recruiting women to keep America humming while they were gone.

"If you've used an electric mixer in your kitchen, you can learn to run a drill press," the government espoused in one campaign poster. Another of my favorite World War II posters shows a woman who looks remarkably like actress Rita Hayworth, clutching love letters to her breast, with a caption that reads, "Longing won't bring him back sooner . . . GET A WAR JOB!" The job of getting women to work was, ironically, the responsibility of the War Manpower Commission.

Women took up the call to action in record numbers. When the United States entered World War II, about twelve million women were in the workforce. By the time the war ended, there were more than eighteen million. Just as important were the jobs they did. Instead of just taking clerical positions or other "traditional female" jobs, women were going into the factories and shipyards and doing the work of men on assembly lines—this time not discouraged by the government or society or men who feared for their jobs, but encouraged by a society that needed and valued their workplace contributions more than ever.

Rosie the Riveter was born.

Created as part of a national marketing and propaganda campaign, Rosie the Riveter posters, songs, and magazine covers would come to represent the changing image of women in the workplace. Millions of American women would venture into the workplace to become real-life "Rosies" and help their country in wartime, swelling the ranks of working women by nearly 60 percent in four years.

The National Parks Service has an excellent exhibit in Richmond, California, and a virtual version on the Internet, which recounts the role of women on the home front during World War II. Part of the presentation includes stories from real-life "Rosies" that paint a realistic picture of the lives and sacrifices they made that one won't typically be found in the patriotic propaganda of the time. Here's a sample from Lucille Sunde, who worked at what was one of the nation's biggest shipyards:

"In March of 1944 I decided to try to get a job working on the Victory ships at Todd Shipyards in Seattle, WA," Sunde writes in a submission on the National Parks site. "It was said it was a patriotic thing to do. Besides, I discovered I was pregnant. My son, Dean, was four years old and payments to the doctor were still owing.

"I was a Rosie the Riveter," she writes. "Most of the time I didn't really know what to do. I worked along with the girls and a team leader. She looked at some plans. Then a big sheet of metal was held up and we attacked it with our rivet guns. I can still hear the sound ringing in my ears. Later some of the holes needed to be reamed out to make them larger.

"My memory of this was what looked like chaos to me," Sunde writes. "There were many hoses laying all around. When I had to walk anywhere on a break or to the rest room, I walked gingerly picking my way through. A story was told about a man who had somehow lost an eye when a powerful air hose burst. Then there were the smells of the metal as it was being worked on. Mixed with the pungent odor of Puget Sound, it made me feel nauseated. The proud feeling of being hired to work on the Victory Ships began to fade to fear on the job and the uncertainty of what I was supposed to do."

Sunde and millions of other Rosies did what they had to do, but as men began to return home from war, the government and media propaganda campaign churned up once again. This time, women were being encouraged to return home and care for their husbands and leave the "real" jobs to them. Men needed their jobs back, and after all that far away fighting in foreign lands, they needed a good woman at home also. Along with the baby boom, the late 1940s brought a new vision of what women should be, epitomized by Debbie Reynolds, Harriet Nelson, and of course Barbara Billingsley, who personified the stereotypical image of the suburban housewife: June Cleaver.

Women, however, didn't buy it hook, line, and sinker like they had before. They had tasted the freedom and the liberation and realized the strength that their work had given them, and they weren't abandoning their newfound roles in the workplace and in society so quickly. After ebbing in the years immediately after World War II, women's participation in the workforce began to grow again in the 1950s. With a new age of consumerism and family growth in America, women often discovered they couldn't quit working. Households were learning for the first time that they needed two paychecks to survive.

In 1957, a Columbia University research group called the National Manpower Council published a seminal study called "Womanpower." It was one of the most comprehensive and important reviews of its time of women's impact on the labor force and their education and employment needs. The report concluded that the government and society in general needed to do more to support women in the workplace to ensure equality, urging the U.S. Secretary of Labor to review its policies toward women. The administration of President Dwight Eisenhower, World War II hero and man-for-all-men, didn't act on the recommendation, however. Women's roles in the workplace and in society continued to remain secondary, often subservient, to men.

And then came the 1960s.

7

Our Turn to Change the World

GAIL COLLINS, the first female editor of *The New York Times*' editorial page, authored two books on women's history, including *When Everything Changed: The Amazing Journey of American Women from 1960 to the Present* (Little, Brown, 2009). In answering the question about how things changed for the better for American women since 1960, Collins wrote: "You can't count the way things are better. Back then, it was perfectly legal to say you weren't hiring a woman or you weren't going to admit her to medical school. In 1960, we had a completely different concept of what was fair. It's way, way, way better in 10 million ways."

When I was in college, there was another book that was all the rage. It was Betty Friedan's 1963 treatise, *The Feminine Mystique* (Norton, 1963). The book had its beginnings in a simple questionnaire Friedan had sent to her fellow Smith College alumnae fifteen years after they graduated. Her findings were so profound that she turned them into a magazine article and then into this groundbreaking book. And then, realizing that writing a book was not enough to change the world for women, Friedan went on to start the National Organization for

Women (NOW), the National Women's Political Caucus, and NARAL, the pro-choice abortion rights group. Interestingly enough, Friedan wrote *The Feminine Mystique* after she got fired from her job as an editor for a newsletter service because she had become pregnant for the third time and her employers didn't want to pay for another maternity leave. She wrote the book in her Rockland County, New York, home while raising her three children, freelancing for magazines, and being a consummate over-educated suburban housewife.

Friedan described what motivated her to write her book and the reaction to it in an interview with the Public Broadcasting Service (PBS) prior to her death in 2006: "After I was fired for being pregnant, I was technically a housewife. And it was (in) the era that I later analyzed, the 'feminine mystique' era (when) 'career woman' was a dirty word," Friedan told PBS. "And so I didn't want a career anymore. (But) I had to do something. So I started freelancing for women's magazines."

In her articles, and later in the book, Friedan defined the 'feminine mystique' as an ideology perpetrated (intentionally, she argued) in the post-World War II period to return women to what a male-dominated society liked to think of as their "dutiful place"—in their traditional roles as mother and wife. The women's adventure of workforce participation during the war was a deviation from the norm. Any woman who resisted the pressure to return to hearth and home was considered abnormal, sick. As a result, Friedan found in her book, women in America were generally unfulfilled, unhappy, and looking for more.

"It was quite fantastic, the effect (the book) had," Friedan told PBS. "It was like I put into words what a lot of women had been feeling and thinking, that they were freaks and they were the only ones. I called my first chapter 'The Problem That Had No Name.' I still meet women all these years later and they say, 'You changed my life or it changed my life,' meaning the book."

I was one of them, and I wasn't alone. Friedan's book would start a new groundswell among women in America. The *New York Times* went so far as to call it one of the most influential nonfiction books of the twentieth century. It "ignited the contemporary women's movement in 1963" and "permanently transformed the social fabric of the United States and countries around the world."

The Feminine Mystique had a profound impact on me. I was one of those women looking to join the workforce around that time. I had no reason to assume I would not be hired back in 1965. I had a management degree from Purdue University. I had grown up in a household where I was repeatedly told I could do anything I set my mind to do. Before I even entered college, my sister and my brother, both older, were already working. My mom had worked, and my dad was a part of our family's business.

So when I hit the pavement to look for a job, I was full of ambition, unafraid, and unaware that anything could hold me back from whatever I wanted to accomplish. Little did I know that I could only interview with companies at my campus job placement agency—Purdue's Career Center for Men—if they specifically said they would interview women. And when I did land an interview, the interviewers looked at my resume and basically said, "We don't know what we would do with a woman with your skills."

Fortunately, two foresighted companies of that time, Arthur Andersen & Co. and IBM, offered me professional positions. My interviewers at Arthur Andersen & Co. had said they would need to ask their clients if they would accept an "Arthur Andersen man in a skirt," and after they did—apparently their clients were willing to take such a progressive risk—they offered me a job.

So the changes that Gail Collins would later write about had started. Not everybody found them like I did, however. Sheila Tobias, author of *Faces of Feminism* (Westview Press, 1997), says of that era: "I personally responded to being of the 'second sex' by leaving the country after graduation from college. In 1963, I had just returned and was trying to figure out why I was not more successful either as a journalist or as a graduate student."

For me, reading *The Feminine Mystique*, the message was loud and clear: The set of beliefs that had begun in the aftermath of World War II and held sway while I was in college did not have to be. Betty

Friedan was basically saying to us: "We should liberate ourselves."

Here are some history-changing moments I remember from the 1960s and beyond:

- Gloria Steinem got her start in the 1960s as a reporter and columnist at *New York* and *Show* magazines, grabbing attention for in-depth stories about women's issues, such as a 1963 investigative report in which she took a job as a "bunny" at a New York *Playboy* club and then wrote an investigative piece about the way she and other "bunnies" were treated. By 1969, Steinem was one of loudest and most influential voices for women's rights in America. In 1971, she would co-found *Ms.* magazine, whose motto today still is "More than a magazine—a movement."

- In 1960 the U.S. Food and Drug Administration gave approval to something called "Enovid" for treatment of menstrual disorder and contraception. The "pill" was born. It would take another four years before a lawsuit in Connecticut would clear the way, allowing oral contraceptives to be sold nationally, but the pill quickly became a necessity for the freedom of women who wanted more than motherhood.

- In 1961, President John F. Kennedy asked former first lady Eleanor Roosevelt to chair the very first Commission on the Status of Women. The Commission was a way to explore issues related to women regarding employment policy, education, and federal laws, and to determine what progress had been made towards giving women "practical equality to men," according to *Time* magazine.

- Newspapers went from having separate "help wanted" columns for women and for men to just one column. Journalists also noticed and protested slanted coverage because of the lack of women in their profession. In 1963, Katharine Graham took over control of the Washington Post Co., becoming one of the most powerful women in the media business. Columnist Erma Bombeck began making her mark, and by 1968, her column that focused on suburban life was syndicated in more than two hundred newspapers. Following Bombeck was Ellen Goodman, who started working at the *Boston Globe* in 1963, and whose columns on women's issues and other topics would later appear in more than three hundred newspapers. On television, Barbara Walters got her start on NBC's "Today" show, and in 1964, she became the show's "Today Girl." Ten years later, Walters would host a daytime talk show, "Not for Women Only," and a few years later, she joined ABC to become the first woman co-anchor of an evening news program.

- In 1964, the Civil Rights Act was enacted, and with it, Title VII, which prohibits discrimination against workers because of race, sex, national origin, or religion.

- I became the first "man in a skirt" at Arthur Andersen & Co., in 1965. Until then, the upper ranks of every accounting and consulting company were the exclusive domain of white men with skinny ties and suits. I remember expecting to be invited to go to lunch with the men. I had a lot of lunches by myself until I took the initiative and started inviting myself to lunch with them.

- Women's professional organizations [e.g., The American Society of Women Accountants (ASWA); The Committee of 200 (C200); the International Women's Forum; and Professional Women's Association of Chicago] allowed women opportunities to have role models and mentors. For the first time, many of us had organized opportunities to learn from other women, including how to network. We also were able to develop and practice our leadership skills in these organizations. I became a member of ASWA, for instance, so I could learn about what accounting firms did. I moved up the ranks to treasurer of the national organization, and soon enough, I was speaking about my career all over the country. Members of these networks became my role models, mentors, and friends. Eventually, some would help me get promoted to partner at Arthur Andersen & Co. Others whom I would mentor would become partners in their own companies.

- Women began supporting other women, creating the woman's liberation movement. Led by Betty Friedan, Kay Clarenbach,

Aileen Hernandez, and others, a few dozen women came together in a hotel room in Washington, D.C., in June 1966 to found what would become the National Organization for Women (NOW). Originally started as a way to pressure the Equal Employment Opportunity Commission (EEOC) to enforce the Title VII mandates in regard to women, the group would grow to more than 500,000 members.

- The Equal Rights Amendment (ERA) movement, which called for changing the U.S. Constitution to guarantee equal rights regardless of sex in any federal, state, or local law, was in full swing. By 1972, ERA got approval in both houses of Congress. But amid protests led by conservative political activist Phyllis Schafly, it failed because it didn't meet a deadline for ratification by three-quarters of the country's state legislatures. Still, the ERA movement is not dead: The amendment has been reintroduced in Congress every year since 1982.

The 1960s would pave the way for so many more accomplishments of women over the next several decades.

Following in the footsteps of Barbara Walters and others, Oprah Winfrey would become the highest-paid television personality ever in 2006. By 2009, news shows would be regularly anchored by women, and the voices of authority that once belonged to the Walter Cronkite, Dan Rather, and Tom Brokaw would be replaced by the likes of Katie Couric, Diane Sawyer, Rachel Maddow, and Christiane Amanpour.

The call for women's rights that echo the ERA movement, the formation of NOW, and so many other political movements are once again heard in new ways. The "women's agendas" of past presidents such as Jimmy Carter, Richard Nixon, Gerald Ford, and Bill Clinton were taken further by President Barack Obama. In his first year in office, Obama created the first White House Commission on Women and Girls and the first office of the Ambassador-at-Large for Global Women's Issues. Melanne Verveer, the first appointee to the ambassadorship, is co-founder of Vital Voices Global Partnership, a nonprofit that works to expand economic opportunities for women worldwide.

In 1972, Congress passed Title IX, prohibiting discrimination of anyone based on sex. Title IX gives equal rights and opportunities to women in academics and athletics. Before Title IX, NCAA-sanctioned women's sports teams were a relative rarity on college campuses. By 2008, a NCAA study found that there were more than 9,000 women's sports teams—more than 8.5 women's teams per school. Nearly 99 percent of colleges had women's basketball teams, according to the study. More than 90 percent had women's volleyball, soccer, and cross-country teams.

Those early writings by Friedan, Steinem, and others paved the way for later journalism and books espousing and encouraging new freedoms for women. In 1989, Felice Schwartz published an article in the *Harvard Business Review* describing what became known as the "Mommy Track" suggesting that businesses needed to be more "family friendly." Her thesis was that companies were losing too many bright female employees, and that it actually cost more to hire women because of their high turnover. Schwartz said there should be more options for women and men. There would be those who wanted to focus on their careers and those who wanted to focus on their family and their career. This became very controversial.

Schwartz said in an interview in *The Boston Globe* in 1992. "What I said was that women face many, many obstacles in the workplace that men do not face. I was saying to that group of men at the top, 'Rather than let women's talents go to waste, do something about it.'"

So, here we are today, taking advantage of what so many have done for us. And what Schwartz pointed out in 1992 still rings true today: There is still more for us to do.

Hopefully, we are moving from the counting the "firsts" for women to becoming women who count. As Betty Friedan wrote, women should liberate themselves. To do so, we need to move beyond simply counting our accomplishments. We need to claim our rightful seats at the world's decision-making tables and begin to make new accomplishments as teams of both women and men. Only then, as equal members, can we make the changes the world needs so badly.

So, how are you going to change the world?

Change Is Happening

8
Change Our Education System

I WAS WRITING this chapter as the 2009 Nobel Prizes were announced in Norway. It was an impressive year for women, with more women among the recipients of the world's highest civilian honors for research and societal contributions than ever before.

With my "counting women" hat on, there were five women among the 2009 Nobel laureates. They won for economics (Elinor Ostrom); literature (Herta Muller); chemistry (Ada Yonath); and medicine (Elizabeth Blackburn and Carol Greider).

The good news is that the 2009 Nobel Prizes showed that women are finally beginning to join in the upper ranks of science and academia. In 2009, 38 percent of the Nobel winners were women. These are women who are truly changing their worlds. Could you imagine if an equal percentage of CEOs, government officials, or other leaders were women?

Education is the key to keep the pipeline flowing and spread the influence of women into those other areas. We need to get more girls more education. And to do that, we have to start early, and we have to start at the very foundations of society.

Women's rights issues are high on many lists these days, from Secretary of State Hillary Rodham Clinton, to the United Nations, to authors Nicholas Kristof and Sheryl WuDunn.

Kristof and WuDunn's 2009 book, *Half the Sky: Turning Oppression into Opportunity for Women Worldwide* (Random House, 2009), outlined the importance of improving the education of women in developing nations to improve their and their countries' opportunities. The authors gave a call for all of us to address women's rights as we hear the cries of oppression from the women and girls they introduce in their book.

After reading many of the women's stories in Kristof and Wu-Dunn's book, I particularly was touched by the story of Saima Muhammad. Saima used to break down into tears every night as she coped with her husband beating her each afternoon, with her house falling apart, and with her daughter forced to live with an aunt because Saima didn't have enough food to feed her. People made fun of Saima. In addition to her husband, her brother-in-law also beat her. Without a grandson, her mother-in-law encouraged her son to find a new wife. After the story got worse, it did get better. Saima signed up with the Kashf Foundation, a Pakistani microfinance organization that gave her a loan and helped teach her how to start her own business making beautiful embroidered cloth. She got her daughter back, she paid off her husband's debts, and now she has members of thirty families working for her, including her husband.

How can we, in Kristof and WuDunn's words, take the "female half" of the population into the world's economy? How can we give them all the same opportunities, the same abilities as the "male half" of the world's population?

Let's look at how some people are doing it:

PAYING RENT FOR LIVING ON THIS EARTH

As a social justice activist who starts programs focused on literacy, closing the achievement gap, and issues of race, Karen Kalish believes this: To whom much is given, much is required.

Karen is the founder of The Teacher Home Visit Program in St. Louis, Missouri. On its surface, the program is simply designed to introduce teachers to the parents/guardians of their students in their home environment, but it does much more than that. The program could be the missing link for a successful education. It fulfills Karen's passion to create a different future for the low-income children in under-performing schools, to end the cycle of poverty, and to level the playing field for African-American children.

When I asked Karen why she had such a passion for inner-city students, she said she is not sure. She feels that doing for others is "the rent we pay for living on this earth."

The education system is broken, Karen says. About 50 percent of the inner-city students drop out of schools. If they do graduate, they typically have an eighth grade reading level. The missing link, according to Karen: Parent/guardian involvement. When Karen sees a problem, she gets two or three allies, rolls up her sleeves, and gets to work finding a solution.

The result: Children who have home visits have higher grades and test scores, better discipline, better attendance, better homework completion rates, and better attitudes toward education.

Nine-year-old Vincent described the impact of having his teachers come to his house: "I'm a better person now because they came over. I now have goals in my life and I have gone from getting Fs to Bs."

Karen "thinks big." She has discovered an opportunity to help a great number of students to be workplace ready or college ready when they graduate from high school. Can you image if the Teacher Home Visit Program was required in every school in the nation? What an impact Karen's program would have on the world.

MENTORS CHANGE LIVES

A mentor changed her life, and now Erin Slater is changing the lives of others. Erin is CEO of College Mentors for Kids, a nonprofit organization that pairs kids in grades 1-8 with college student mentors who expose them to the opportunities that can come with higher education.

Erin lost her mother in a car accident when she was five. Her dad passed away when she was sixteen. By the time she finally graduated from high school (a little late, she would admit), she was a mess. Purdue University rejected her because of her grades. Her life was in shambles.

She began waiting tables at a restaurant and thought that maybe she would own a restaurant one day. And then a woman who had been a mentor in the College Mentors for Kids program came into her life. She convinced Erin to think about getting into school again. Erin went to a community college to complete the basic courses. She reapplied to Purdue, and this time, she got in.

During the mentoring program, the kids learn all about college buildings, living at school, professors, majors, and diplomas. They explore what they want to be and what they need to do to get into college—all of this by the time they graduate from the eighth grade. The result: They constantly talk about going to college, they see themselves as college students, they want to be like their mentors, and they have a different attitude about going to school.

The mentors themselves become rising leaders in the program and on campus. Stephanie, one mentor who was thinking about dropping out of college, decided to stay. How could she tell her buddies to go to college when she was not setting an example herself? Many become education majors, wanting to take their newfound teaching skills even further. Some join Teach for America, a program that enlists future leaders to be teachers for two years in the highest-need schools around the country.

Erin is "thinking big" about expanding the program because she knows the impact of College Mentors on the kids, the parents/guardians, their families, and their communities to a future they might never have known. Others, like Martha Stewart, know the difference that Erin is making. Erin was recently the winner of Martha Stewart's 2009 Dreamers into Doers award.

COLLEGE PREPARATION FOR WOMEN, BY WOMEN

There's a particular part of our declining education system that is perhaps the most troubling. Educators and policy makers refer to it as STEM—science, technology, engineering, and mathematics. Simply put, our young people are not graduating with the STEM skills necessary to be the next generation of inventors, creators, and groundbreaking scientists—the next leaders of the twenty-first century.

In 2000, Joan Hall helped create a public charter school, the Young Women's Leadership Charter School (YWLCS) in Chicago. To Joan, it was her answer to preparing under-served female students to graduate from high school, excel in college, and lead productive and fulfilling lives. She has found an educational model for these young girls to say, "It's cool to be smart." The students, who are in grades 7-12, embark on a rigorous college preparation curriculum based on science, math, and technology. By 2009, over 90 percent of the class graduated and over 85 percent were accepted to college.

When La Shenna Clark was in the seventh grade, her teacher told her about YWLCS. With her mother, La Shenna met with Joan. She fell in love with the school and its mission and vision. She was hooked. With her mom and founder Joan in her corner, La Shenna discovered the doors to go through to excel and expand her options, and she went to college. After a difficult freshman year, La Shenna was really pleased with herself. "I even graduated on time (four years)," she told me. She is a determined young woman and is now studying to get a graduate degree in marriage and family counseling. What makes the Young Women's Leadership Charter School so special? With roughly fifty girls in each class in grades 7-12, students and their parents learn two things very quickly: They learn to believe in themselves, and they learn the value of hard work.

LAUNCHING TOMORROW'S LEADERS

Meet Dr. France Córdova, president of Purdue University.

In 1969, the world was watching Neil Armstrong (a Purdue graduate) take his first steps onto the moon. Among those glued to their television was France Córdova, a newly-minted Stanford University graduate with an English degree. She was inspired by the nation's response to Sputnik and the race to put a man on the moon—so much so, that she changed her career path and earned a PhD in physics. She spent many years researching astrophysics at Los Alamos National Laboratory, became the first female chief scientist at NASA, and eventually was selected as the first woman president of Purdue University.

Dr. Córdova is the oldest of twelve children and was born in Paris, France. "When I went to school, teachers felt certain studies—like physics—were only for boys," she told me. "Girls didn't go to graduate school. And, if you went to college, you got married afterwards. In fact, my mother told me the most important degree to earn in college was a 'Mrs.' degree!"

Dr. Córdova works directly with her students to enhance their academic excellence and leadership potential. She encourages them to become leaders from the moment they step onto campus as freshmen. She particularly wants to attract more students into careers in science and engineering, believing that it is such fields that can keep our nation innovative and competitive globally.

Dr. Córdova wants students to develop their math and science skills early, so she has encouraged Purdue's interest in providing more qualified science and math teachers in the K-12 classrooms. To support this focus, Purdue is a part of the Woodrow Wilson Indiana Teaching Fellow Program, which will send specially trained math and science teachers into Indiana rural schools to strengthen STEM instruction. Dr. Córdova hopes this will increase the pipeline of students interested and prepared in math and science.

With her background as a scientist, Dr. Córdova is also passionate about increasing the number of women and underrepresented minorities in the STEM disciplines. She wants them to be prepared for what she knows personally to be exciting careers—as professors, university administrators, government advisors, and policy leaders—and be prepared to impact critical issues like education, energy, the environment, health, and security.

Dr. Córdova has certainly been one of those "change agents" for women—in fact, for all students—with her focus on "Launching Tomorrow's Leaders."

CREATING IMPACTFUL EXPERIENCES

Speaking of launches, another important person we all know as the first American woman in space is Sally Ride. Did you know she left college to pursue a professional career in tennis? When tennis didn't work out as planned, she went back to Stanford University and earned several degrees, including a postdoctorate in astrophysics.

As a result, Dr. Ride had a successful career as an astronaut and helped change the opportunities for women in the field of aerospace. Now, she is trying to influence even more young girls and get them excited about science. Dr. Ride provides them the opportunity to experience science personally at her Sally Ride Science Camps.

When she was in the eighth grade in Indianapolis, Reedi Garrett attended a Sally Ride-sponsored camp at Stanford University. She told me it was a life-changing experience. When Reedi went to the camp, it was her first plane ride and her first trip to California. She was away from home for the first time, living on a college campus. Once at camp, she spent the days doing hands-on experiments. She particularly remembers the "build your dream home" project. The assignment was to create a blueprint and then build a house with construction paper, wooden sticks, and glue. In reflecting on this later, she found she liked the "hands-on" part of what she later would discover to be a simple form of engineering.

The camp wasn't all about engineering and science. There was the talent show that helped Reedi get comfortable with some of the girls and step out of her normal comfort zone. And then there was the nature walk at night where she had to walk a small section by herself. She felt that if she could walk by herself in California in the dark woods, she could do anything.

Meg Whitman, then the CEO of eBay, also talked to the girls about the importance of being a leader and described her experiences running the giant Internet auction site. Lastly, Reedi felt very special and important when she saw Sally Ride and received a signed picture.

What was the result of that week? Reedi graduated from high school and went on to study mechanical engineering technology at Purdue. By the time she was a junior, she had many work experiences and had already accepted an offer of employment for a job she will start after graduation.

With her camp, Dr. Ride is doing her part to turn the tide and to increase the number of young girls like Reedi who are studying STEM-related courses. She's getting them excited about science and engineering and prepping them to change our world.

IT'S COOL TO BE SMART

Attorney-educator Joann DiGennaro co-founded the Center for Excellence in Education (CEE) in McLean, Virginia, with Admiral Hyman Rickover. Joann's desire is to find the brightest students in science and technology, and nurture their minds to be creators, innovators, scientists, Nobel Prize winners, and leaders of the twenty-first century. She believes that nurturing these students is essential to keep the United States competitive and to further international understanding.

The programs for the students are free and lead to significant opportunities for them as they pursue their undergraduate and graduate schooling. As part of CEE's Research Science Institute, fifty of the brightest high school students from the United States and twenty-five to thirty from other countries are selected (from more than twenty thousand applicants) to spend six weeks doing research with Massachusetts Institute of Technology professors. About 40 percent are women, primarily Asians, Latinas, and Native Americans. They become a very close-knit group. They are pushed to go to college, participate in competitions, and work toward STEM-related careers.

Pam Krahl was in one of the early CEE programs. She found out about the program when she was a junior in high school, after her mother saw a story about it in the newspaper. Pam applied, was accepted, and spent six weeks the following summer with classroom education and interning with a scientist. It would set the path for the rest of Pam's life. She went on to graduate from the U.S. Naval Academy, went to medical school, and is now Dr. Pam Krahl of the U.S. Navy.

Finding young students like Pam who think it is cool to be smart is what CEE is about, says Joann. We all need to develop the minds of students to be scientists, innovators, scientists, and Nobel Prize winners.

TEACHING WOMEN TO BE ENTREPRENEURS

Accenture has always helped nonprofit organizations in cities where it has operations. For example, employees volunteer to help inner-city children learn computer skills or may volunteer in the classroom for Junior Achievement (JA) to teach students in grades K-12 to be better citizens of their communities, and to be workplace ready.

When Amy Loftus, a senior executive at Accenture, gets up in the morning, she often thinks, "How am I going to make a difference today?" By the end of the day, she thinks, "How did I make a difference today with everyone that I touched?" One day, Amy thought about how Accenture's Women's Network could really make a difference for young women in Philadelphia.

Based on her office's experience with JA, Amy and others in Accenture's Women's Network teamed up with the Philadelphia public school system and JA to offer the JA Company Program to local girls. Through the program, students learn how to organize and operate an actual business. It is a real entrepreneurial experience. They learn how a business functions, about the structure of the U.S. free enterprise system, and how to make money. The women served as role models and advisors to fourteen girls as they progressed through the eight-month, two-hours-per-week program. Amy told me it was amazing when the students learned leadership principles, corporate organization, product development, sales and marketing. They also learned to analyze data, negotiate, develop reports, give talks, and work as a team.

The girls decided they wanted to get into the T-shirt business. They designed their own shirts, and then learned how to produce them, price them, and sell them. When we talked, Amy was reminded of one of the girls who sold twelve T-shirts at $9 each. She was beaming from ear to ear when she came to the class that night. It was a big accomplishment. At the end of the program, with the girls wearing the T-shirts they created, they gave talks about what they had accomplished with their company. As with many others who have completed the JA Company Program, this was a defining point in their young lives. The girls learned to be entrepreneurs and demonstrated success with their ideas and abilities to create a successful company. Based on the success of this program, Amy is now working on ways that Accenture could make an even bigger impact in Philadelphia.

LEARNING TO LEAD WITH INTEGRITY

Carla Paonessa, a retired senior executive from Accenture, is relentlessly curious. She wonders about things like what makes some relationships work and others not. She wonders what happens inside someone's heart/head that influences what they do and how they behave. She likes to explore how leaders really lead.

Knowing her interests, a colleague suggested to Carla that she check out The LeaderShape Institute, a six-day program designed to help participants learn how to "lead with integrity." Participants achieve four primary outcomes: They increase their commitment to acting consistently with core ethical values, personal values, and convictions; they increase their capability to develop and enrich relationships as well as to increase their commitment to respecting the dignity and contribution of all people; they learn to embrace the belief in a healthy disregard for the impossible; and they develop the capability to produce extraordinary results.

Carla tells this story: "At the end of the six days, I observed fifteen members in my 'family cluster' shed tears—including me—over the experience they had that week. They interacted with people of different colors, different cultures, different social privileges, different sexual persuasions, and they concluded they were all one family. A fraternity jock from California said: 'I've never experienced this much fun without alcohol, ever.' Actually, those students experienced the 'high' of authentic relationships. Authenticity will do it to you every time. It will let you touch the soul of the universe and make you weep."

People cite different students who have been through LeaderShape. Larry Page, co-founder of Google, is a graduate of LeaderShape. At the 2009 commencement address Page delivered at the University of Michigan, he said he was at LeaderShape when he started dreaming about a search engine that could find anything when asked.

After retiring from Accenture, Carla joined the faculty of Leader-Shape. Now, she's a member of its board of trustees. She invests her time in LeaderShape because she wants to help students learn how to "show up real" in every moment of their lives and live and lead with integrity. This needs to happen throughout the world. If we could do that, we would bring about mass changes in the world in just one generation.

TEACHING SELF-CONFIDENCE

Her obituary called her "a fearless warrior for the voiceless." Eunice Shriver spent her life championing the rights of the intellectually disabled, beginning with her own sister. In doing so, Shriver brought people with special needs into the mainstream and educated others around the world about their potential.

Shriver's sister, Rosemary, suffered from mental illness and was possibly slightly retarded. In an effort to cure her, doctors performed a lobotomy when she was twenty-three that caused permanent brain damage. Rosemary Shriver spent the rest of her life in an institution. Rather than hide her sister's condition—as was the norm of the time—Eunice Shriver brought it out into the open, revealing it during brother's campaign for president.

Later, as executive vice president of the Joseph P. Kennedy, Jr. Foundation in the 1950s, Eunice Shriver focused her father's nonprofit foundation to support research on mental retardation. In 1968, melding the foundation's research with her love of sports and athletics, Shriver teamed up Anne McGlone, a Chicago-area physical education teacher (who would later become an Illinois Supreme Court judge) to sponsor what was expected to be a one-time competition event for special needs athletes. The event would become the foundation for the Special Olympics, which today has more than three million participants in 175 countries.

When she died in August 2009, Shriver's family issued a statement recalling her "as a champion for people with intellectual disabilities and as an extraordinary woman who, as much as anyone, taught our nation—and our world—that no physical or mental barrier can restrain the power of the human spirit."

Shriver followed her passion, educated the world about something that it needed to learn. Along the way, she changed the world.

HELPING A SON, HELPING THE WORLD

Vanessa Truett, from Springfield, Oregon, is a young woman with a special passion.

"Our oldest son Geronimo has an autism diagnosis," Vanessa told me. "When you have a baby, the first thing someone says is 'Does he have ten fingers and toes?' You aren't told, 'He looks fine, but somewhere in the next two years he will regress and no longer meet all those developmental milestones you read about.'"

Vanessa went on. "One day we realized he was not talking. He did not seek to share information with us, he jumped up and down and flapped his arms while humming. My son could arrange the alphabet blocks in order and point to the isosceles trapezoid. He was three and had never said 'Mama.' He had never even looked me in the eye."

Vanessa's mother, my cousin Jane Eyre McDonald, happened to write her thesis in graduate school on autism. And Vanessa's background includes activism for the disabled or underrepresented. This all helped the family cope with Geronimo's autism. In the past few years, they are not only learning how to develop his potential, but to help others who find themselves in a similar situation.

Today, Vanessa writes grants for autism research. She assists in large-scale fund-raising events for their local autism organization. She blogs about autism, develops e-mail campaigns, and participates in

Springfield's "Warm Line," a program through which supporters call a family after their child receives an "autism-like" diagnosis.

Vanessa, too, is changing the world in her own way, by educating others about autism through her blogs, grant writing, and fundraising.

Let's go back to Nobel Laureate Elinor Ostrom for a moment.

There are many factors that contributed to her success, but none more than a good education. In an interview with the *Indianapolis Star* newspaper as she prepared to accept the 2009 Nobel Prize for economics, Ostrom recounted just how important education was to her.

She grew up in a poor family in Los Angeles during the end of the Great Depression. Her father was an artist, but he had to take a job laying bricks because it was the only work he could find. Most of the family's food came from their garden. Despite the hardship, Ostrom's mother had the foresight to lobby local school officials for a waiver to get young Elinor into the best school district in the region, Beverly Hills. The school system was rich in resources and one where the entire student body was expected to go to college. Ostrom later called her transfer into the prestigious school system life-changing.

"I would not have gone to college without being in that environment," she told the *Indianapolis Star*. "My mom had no more than high school, and my dad had no more than high school. Neither saw college as being important. But I went (to college) because all my friends were going."

What would have become of Ostrom if her mother had not pushed to get her into the best school district she could find? What would have happened to Saima Muhammad if she had not received educational and financial help from the Kashf Foundation, as detailed in Kristof's and WuDunn's *Half the Sky*? What would have become of Erin Slater if she had not received guidance from the College Mentors for Kids program that she now runs? How many girls like La Shena Clark, of the Young Women's Leadership Charter School in Chicago, are we reaching, and how many are falling through the cracks of our education system today?

Women like these and so many more are changing the world, one little corner at a time, through education and because of education.

Changing the world with education doesn't mean we have to completely remake our school system, or that you need to become a university president or even a certified teacher. Changing the world with education means using your situation along with your talents, your skills, and your gifts to educate others in ways that make the world a better place.

9
Change Our Organizations

THE YEARS 2008-2009 were a time of great change in America, but not necessarily for women in the top ranks of business and industry.

The numbers tell the story. A 2009 report by The White House Project, a nonpartisan, nonprofit group created to help women get into leadership roles in politics and elsewhere, showed that women accounted for 46 percent of the workforce and 51 percent of the managerial/administrative/professional positions in America. Yet of the 10 industry sectors that the report focused on, women held only 18 percent of the top leadership positions. Among Fortune 500 companies, women constituted 3 percent of the CEOs, 6 percent of the top-paying positions and 16 percent of the corporate officers.

Of course women are making some inroads into top leadership roles. In 2009, Ursula Burns replaced Anne Mulcahy at Xerox—becoming the first black woman CEO to run a Fortune 500 company and the first woman to replace another member of her gender on the Fortune 500 list.

But consider those numbers from The White House Project again in this way: Women make up nearly half of the nation's workforce (and they also represent more than half of nation's buying power, by the way), yet they represent less than one-fifth of the top leadership at American companies and only 3 percent of CEOs at the nation's Fortune 500 companies.

It's time for us women to take responsibility for these numbers and begin to change them. Given the problems facing our organizations and our world, we can't wait for others, we can't wait for more laws, we can't wait for more numbers. We must do it ourselves, and we must do it now.

Pontish Yeramyan, founder and CEO of the consulting company Gap International, perhaps puts it best in her company's inspirational slogan and her personal goal: "Transform Organizations—Transform the World."

Never before has there been a better time for women to be the drivers of transformation, in their organizations and in the world. It's our time to shine, if we only choose to take up the challenge.

Now think of your own organization and your own career, and consider these questions:

- Are you developing your career path so you demonstrate the skills and capabilities of the position you aspire to obtain?
- Do you have an advocate who pushes you beyond your comfort zone so others can see your potential?
- Are you visible in your organization?
- Have you asked for or applied for the position that you want— even before you believe you are well prepared for it?
- Does your organization have a succession plan? Are you on it? Will it get you to where you aspire to be?
- Are you developing your replacement by giving her the right roles and responsibilities, no matter what level you are in your organization?
- Are you providing her the right visibility to be ready for your position?

Why are more women needed in top roles in our companies and organizations? Consider the discussion at the January 2009 annual meeting of the World Economic Forum. The meeting was held in

Davos, Switzerland, just as the world was struggling with the worst financial industry meltdown in recent history. Participants were asked a seemingly pithy but surely pertinent question: "Would we be in this mess if it were the Lehman Sisters (instead of Lehman Brothers)?"

The responses were quite telling. The consensus was that more "sisters" would have saved the world from the corrosive gambling culture that dominated many a trading room. Here are some excerpts from the *New York Times* and the *International Herald Tribune*:

Neelie Kroes, the European Union's Commissioner of Competition, said she "was absolutely" convinced that testosterone was one of the reasons the financial system had been brought to its knees. "In general terms, females are a bit less ego-driven and a bit more responsible than men," she said.

Muhammad Yunus, the Nobel-winning microfinance pioneer whose Grameen Bank in Bangladesh lends to women rather than men, said the current crisis would almost certainly not have happened if women had shaped financial practices rather than men. "Women are more cautious," he said. "They wouldn't have taken the enormous types of risks that brought the system down."

Kenneth Rogoff, a Harvard economist, recalled that it was German Chancellor Angela Merkel who had eighteen months ago called for transparency in financial markets and regulation of the non-bank financial sector. "She didn't even want heavy regulation, she was just completely sane and sensible—but she was squashed by all the men," Rogoff said. "She was a lone voice and that's the problem. We need more gender diversity in the finance sector."

Laura Liswood, secretary general of the Council of Women World Leaders said: "Ideally, it will be Lehman Brothers and Sisters in the future. The finance system of the future would have just as many women as men, to combine the more female tendency to be responsible and forward-looking with the male tendency to take risks."

I love that idea. That's true teamwork—teams that "are balanced by gender and therefore balance risk-taking with responsibility for the present and the future." Think about how the world could change for the better if all our organizations had such teams.

Despite the sentiment at the World Economic Forum, though, its make-up was telling of our world today. Of the eighty high-powered financial leaders from around the globe, only six were women. According to the *New York Times*, they all were sitting in one corner of the room.

DEVELOPING MORE SISTERS

The vision for the future is that we need more "sisters" everywhere in our organizations—"sisters" who will combine the female tendency to be responsible and forward-looking with the male tendency to take risks.

With more "sisters" we will have different ways of looking at problems, more diversity of thought. More women on corporate boards will yield more women as corporate officers. Mentoring programs will be a priority, and human resources departments will rethink policies to be more family-friendly. Succession planning should be in place, and we move forward from being tokens to a critical mass where our voices will be heard.

Won't it be truly remarkable when we have so many women in leadership roles, including CEOs and directors, that we don't need to count women anymore? I am hoping it will be in my lifetime.

So how are we going to make it happen?

First, women themselves need to do more to get women to the top of organizations. At all levels, we need to support one another, proactively develop and promote women on our own teams, be their advocates, and help them get the visibility they need. When I ask women why there aren't more women in the senior ranks of any organization, the answer I frequently hear is, "The woman at the top likes being the only woman." They are not helping others climb the career ladder and join them in leading the organization to new heights. Others say, "I did it on my own merit, so others can too." Actually none of us— women or men—made it to the top on our own.

If we are truly interested in our future and in being a part of our organization's success, we should all want more women at all levels of our organization. Research has demonstrated that in companies with women at all levels, returns are better, shareholder value is higher, and employees are happier. And if we don't hire and grow these very talented women, our organizations will be losing out on a significant pool of talent.

I believe women need to be woven throughout the fabric of any organization that cares about success. In a company, women should comprise at least 30-40 percent of working committees at all levels, the senior ranks, and the important income-generating jobs of the corporation. Additionally, since women comprise more than 50 percent of the working population, we should be developing women to be at least 30-40 percent of all levels in the organization. This will provide more opportunities for women to seek higher-level positions.

Companies themselves need to realize that it is in their own best interest to adopt a "women-friendly" culture, which can bring about better decisions (just ask the World Economic Forum participants) and deliver more value to the bottom line. This includes such proactive activities as mentorship, career opportunities that allow access to more senior positions, family-friendly policies with more flexibility, and evaluation criteria based on the value the individual delivers.

Women need to have mentors and strong advocates who will push them to excel. And all women need to realize that they have this same responsibility to be a mentor and advocate for other women. More experienced women also need to let younger women have a chance to spread their wings and lead.

I like the strategy of the National Association of Female Executives and its goal to significantly expand and improve the pipeline to the executive suite by recruiting, developing, and promoting women from entry-level jobs on up. The organization annually identifies the top companies for female executives by using the following criteria:

1. There are at least two women on the board of directors.
2. Women are common in senior ranks—running departments and divisions, reporting directly to the CEO, and participating in corporate succession plans.

3. The company's executive team is aimed at helping women to be successful at all levels of the company.
4. Women are engaged and part of the corporate culture.
5. Women are rewarded by showing the value they deliver to the company.
6. Women's voices are heard.

We should all want to have our companies on this group's Top 10 list. Does your organization meet these requirements? What might you be able to do to help make change happen so it would qualify?

Boston Consulting Group (BCG) is a company worth examining. When Hans-Paul Burkner became CEO in 2003, he vowed to recruit and retain women. Six years later, the firm had three women on its thirteen-person executive committee, and one-third of its consultants were women.

His organization has definitely become more "women friendly." In 2009 it was ranked number three among *Fortune* magazine's "Best Companies to Work For." What has BCG done to propel itself to the top tier of that list?

- It values the skills that women bring to the table and uses them to build the client base, particularly in areas where the client base is predominantly women.
- Women are coached to build skills, and mentors provide "off the record" advice.
- It gives flexibility to women with children. At BCG, you can be both a mother and a partner.
- It has an annual women's conference focused on career development.

What do forward-thinking companies like BCG and Gap International have in common? I have observed the following:

- Leaders have courage and are deliberate about developing people, especially women.
- Talents are identified and given opportunities.
- Diversity is a part of the culture.
- Leaders promote a "talent mentality." There are rewards and recognition for doing a great job.

- Women and diverse suppliers are a part of the culture.
- Voices are heard, and diversity is in the pipeline.

Think about that in the context of companies and other organizations, then think about how our world can change if we change our organizations. If company leaders promote diversity and increase the ranks of women in their top management, those top managers will in turn promote diversity and women who work for them. Just like at Xerox, women will more commonly replace women in the CEO suite. As that happens, women will encourage—better yet, insist—that their suppliers and partners also consider diversity and women.

The net result? We will have not just "brothers" like the Lehmans making decisions; we will also have "sisters" included in the process. And if brilliant thinkers like those at the World Economic Forum are right, including more "sisters" will make companies, organizations, industries, countries, and the world a better place.

CHANGE OUR ORGANIZATIONS, CHANGE OUR WORLD.

So what to do? We need to help our organizations transform themselves. Here are some steps to take right now in your organization:

- Understand where women are—and aren't—in your organization.
- Identify where women could have larger roles in your organization, and help define ways to get them in these key positions.
- Develop ways to increase the number of women at all levels.
- Ensure that women are visible in the organization, on committees, involved in decisions, etc.
- Use women in the organization as change agents, to help other women move up in the organization.
- Encourage women to serve as mentors to other women.
- Get more women into the executive pipeline. If we do that, more will eventually make it into the executive suite, perhaps even the CEO's office.

- Have a plan in place with purposeful accomplishments for you and the company. Take time to build purposeful relationships.
- Stand up and let your voice be heard. And make sure your voice counts.

Take these steps and you can change your organization. Change your organization, and you can change the world.

10
Change Our Communities

WHEN I WAS GROWING UP, my parents always seemed busy doing something in our community. For my dad, it was Rotary Club and all of its service projects, the American Red Cross and all of its campaigns and blood drives, and the city council with all of its meetings. My uncle and family friends were mayors of our little town. And my mother, when she wasn't taking food to the church, running the church nursery, or working at the Red Cross, was shuttling needy friends and neighbors to the doctor, helping them figure out their finances, or running errands for them. She later worked at the library, using her wonderful secretarial skills (she was the first person I knew who could write in shorthand), handling books, and helping patrons.

More recently, my friend Barrett's son, Alex Avigdor, went to a small community in the Dominican Republic with a group called "Amigos de las Americas." There, he helped construct benches at a bus stop. He put trashcans in the streets and organized trash collection. He ran camps for school children. Through his community service he was able to change this small community. The benches provided safety for the older adults, and the garbage collection supported a healthier environment.

We all saw the outpouring of support for Haiti after the horrible January 2010 earthquake there.

The world may have gotten a lot smaller, but the driving force behind my parents, behind Alex, and behind all the volunteers who helped Haiti remains the same: Community service makes a difference, no matter where you are or what you're doing. Just like changing your organization, changing your community changes the world.

The problems of our world community aren't confined just to developing and third-world countries. On the eve of Thanksgiving 2009, the U.S. Department of Agriculture reported that nearly 15 percent of American households, including nearly a fourth of the nation's children, struggled to get enough to eat for at least part of the previous year. This was the highest level since the government began tracking what it calls "food insecurity." A congressional hearing a day later put another face on the problem: Community food banks around the country reported that they were seeing record increases in demand and record declines in donations. Leaders of food banks said they had to turn people away because they didn't have enough food to give to the needy or enough people to help distribute the items. Middle-class moms and dads who had once served as volunteers at their community food banks suddenly found themselves on the other side of the line, needing a hand from others.

"In a nation that has so much, this is not right," U.S. Representative John Lewis, the civil rights icon turned congressman, said at the hearing. "It is not just. It is not fair. We can and we must find a way to do better."

We can do better, by helping our communities in any and every way we can. Along with lack of food, too many people still are homeless, jobless, and friendless. They need our help.

I remember when my company first stressed the importance of "giving back." The idea that stuck with me was that the people in the city where I lived helped make my company profitable and helped pay my salary, so I should support them, too. There was clear incentive to volunteer in the community, because without the community, my company might not exist. I learned the importance of giving back (or as I like to say it, "giving forward") and making my community a better place for my having been there.

Volunteering is a way to invest your time, talents, and resources and to encourage the spirit of service. Why is "giving forward" particularly important for women? First, there are so many women and girls, not living very far from each of us, who will never be able to achieve their dreams if someone doesn't provide them a "nudge," and/or a helping hand to have a better life. That nudge can come in myriad ways: Volunteering with the Girl Scouts, spending a day in the classroom for a Junior Achievement program, being a Big Sister to a girl who needs a role model.

Another way to "give forward" to change your community is to use your own passions to help others. This not only provides help to people who need it most, it also helps you hone your skills and learn a little more about what you love to do most. Like writing? Help out with the community newsletter or church bulletin. Don't mind driving? Volunteer at Meals on Wheels. Have a passion for cooking? Help out preparing dinners at a community shelter. Who knows the impact you can make, just by doing what you love to do.

Earlier, I mentioned my friend Tamara who started a nonprofit group called Live Love Now. Her idea was big but simple: Encourage people to do everything they do out of love. With partner Misty Miller, one of the first things Tamara's group did was host a Valentine's Day community benefit concert in San Diego. Enlisting the help of Misty's husband, a local musician, the two women began contacting other musicians throughout Southern California to see what it would cost for them to play at the event. Every musician they contacted said they would play—and play for free as their way to "live love." Attendees discovered a great way to celebrate Valentine's Day. The musicians had a blast, jamming together and enjoying their passions. Tamara and Misty gave all the proceeds to breast cancer research. What Tamara and Misty did was find a way to tap into their passions—helping others and living love—and also tap into the passions of musicians, all for the good of the community—and for a good time.

You don't have to put on a concert just to give back to your community. Little things can make just as big a difference to people who need help. I remember one Sunday afternoon when my cousin came into the assisted-living facility where my mother lived and sat down at the piano. She played tunes that the women knew. Suddenly the women, some whom were typically silenced by Alzheimer's and other diseases, sat up and began singing. They sang and sang and sang that day. Are animals your thing? Just like music, pets can put a big smile on the faces of these residents. Who would have thought that you could brighten up your community just by taking your dog for a walk?

There is an outlet for every passion. The Women's Foundation of Southern Arizona is one of hundreds of women's funds working globally to create a world where women and girls are able to achieve their full potential and pursue their dreams. The Women's Foundation compiles research on issues and challenges affecting women and girls, funding programs that create social change to address those challenges. The award-winning girls' philanthropy program Unidas teaches teen girls leadership, philanthropy, and social justice through hands-on grant-making. Unidas participants inspire change in the community and in each other. Gifts of time, talent, and resources in such programs change our community and our women and girls.

Another group I'm involved in is Girl Scouts of the USA, having served on its national board. Girl Scouting, of course, is a big part of millions of young girls' lives, from Daisies to Ambassador Girl Scouts. At a national Girl Scout meeting I attended a young Native American girl told about her Girl Scout experience. At the beginning, she said, she was unable to communicate with the other girls in her troop, because she spoke Native American English. Now she was going to become a doctor and go back to her reservation and help sick people. She attributed her aspirations to her experiences with the Girl Scouts.

Today's Girl Scout program is changing. It is focusing on building teen leaders all across America to become change-makers, envisioning that they could implement short-term community programs. By learning leadership, problem-solving, and entrepreneurial skills, the Girl Scouts are working in their communities, making a difference.

Lisa Reither is a former senior Girl Scout and Accenture executive. Now her family runs the Deer Valley YMCA Family Camp near

Pittsburgh. Among other things, the camp hosts special programs for women—from quilting groups to "Women's Weeks" that feature everything from lectures on leadership to spa days. Lisa and her family had attended the Deer Valley Family Camp for more than fifteen years, and they learned firsthand the difference it made in their lives and in the lifeblood of their community. Now Lisa is giving forward by helping create valuable and special experiences for others through camp programs.

I once asked Lisa: If you won the lottery, what would you do? Her answer: "I would definitely leave Accenture in order to go to work part-time for a nonprofit organization where I could make a difference to others in need." Even though she didn't win the lottery she decided to do exactly what she wanted to do: live her passion by working for a nonprofit and make a difference in her community.

For most of us, it doesn't take winning the lottery to live the life of our dreams. It just takes courage.

Running for office is another way that courageous women can make their communities better. The United States ranks seventy-first in the world when it comes to the number of women holding elected office. Bolivia has more women in parliamentary positions than we do. El Salvador has nearly as many. We are behind the United Kingdom, Japan, France, and many other world powers. While women make up more than half of the population in the United States, they make up only 17 percent of the Congress that represents all of us. Clearly, we need more women in all levels of public office, from the smallest of city councils to the halls of Congress.

The White House Project is opening doors for thousands of women who want to run for political office. Organization founder Marie Wilson and her staff host programs like Go Run! that teach participants the nuts-and-bolts of running for office and how to have a life in politics. Programs and support systems are available to you if you are interested in running for office. The time has never been better to do so.

"From now on, it will be unremarkable for a woman to win primary state victories, unremarkable to have a woman in a close race to be our nominee, unremarkable to think that a woman can be the president of the United States. And that is truly remarkable," says Hillary Rodham Clinton, Secretary of State and presidential candidate.

Holding public office—whether paid or unpaid—is of course a real commitment to making change happen. As I look in my own community, there are many women who are already elected, and many more who are running to be elected.

Clinton's rise reminds us of another community not to be forgotten—the international community. As Secretary of State, Clinton has made women's rights one of her signature issues. As columnist Ellen Goodman put it: "Clinton's role is a boon for women around the world." In her push to improve the social and political status of women, Secretary Clinton says, "Democracy means nothing if half of the people can't vote, or if their vote doesn't count, or if their literacy rate is so low that the exercise of their vote is in question. The transformation of women's roles is the last great impediment to universal progress."

Kathy Calvin is chief operating officer and executive vice president of the United Nations Foundation, a public charity started with an act of philanthropy—media mogul Ted Turner's $1 billion gift. Kathy shared with me the focus of the U.N. and the foundation when it comes to women's rights: To create an impactful agency to support the advancement of women around the world and support the struggle for women's equality and rights. The United Nations Foundation, along with the U.N., is making the case that world leaders should invest in the future of women and girls.

To share some statistics, three-fifths of the world's poorest people are women and girls; 70 percent of the children not in school are girls; half a million women die every year in childbirth. Clearly, by focusing on women's issues, we can help stability, security, and equity around the world. We can change the world.

Again, I ask you: Where will you invest your time to make an impact in your community, whether it is where you live or on the other side of the world?

Go for it.

11
Change Our Giving

IT WAS A MYSTERY that captured the attention of the media and the world of philanthropy.

Someone, somewhere, was changing the world through his or her anonymous donations to schools of higher education across America. Through April 2009, nearly $70 million poured into at least thirteen colleges and universities across the country from a single anonymous donor or group of donors, according to the Associated Press. The one common thread: All of the money went to schools led by female presidents. Speculation abounded as to the identity of the donor or donors. Maybe the money came from a famous celebrity, such as Oprah Winfrey? Or perhaps it came from a woman who grew up at a time when going to college wasn't taken for granted? Maybe it came from someone who recognized that in order to change the world, we need women at the top management positions, universities included? Perhaps by remaining anonymous the mystery donor (or donors) just wanted to encourage others to give too, not for notoriety or for recognition, but just because it's the right thing to do and an important way to change the world?

Whatever the motivation, the mystery donor had a focus for his or her giving, knew how much they wanted to give, and how it should be used.

The donor was really giving to make a difference, to make change happen.

Are you giving in a purposeful way to make specific change happen in your community or in the world? Are you giving in a way that spurs others into action?

Although we are changing, women typically have had a very different giving pattern than men. Since we have a hard time saying "no" to anyone, we have a real tendency to give our money to a lot of organizations and consequently give smaller amounts of money. And in many cases, we do not consider what we want to see happen as a result of the donation. Men typically do just the opposite, giving more to fewer causes and probably saying "no" more often.

From my standpoint, I have changed over time, from giving small amounts to a lot of organizations, to giving more targeted amounts to two or three organizations. By doing so, I can support the philanthropies that receive my money in a bigger way and help them achieve specific goals. The organizations also appreciate bigger donations. I believe that it is important to give in a meaningful and more focused way, rather than giving a few dollars to everyone who knocks on my door.

Eli Broad, the real estate magnate who started KB Home and the financial services firm Sun America, perhaps put it best in an August 2009 interview with the *Wall Street Journal*. According to the article, "Mr. Broad says he is not in the 'check-writing charity business. We're in the venture philanthropy business.' Which is to say, he wants to see results. Even in areas that are outside what he really knows, he has found people he trusts to give him advice on where his money can have the greatest impact. He's given hundreds of millions of dollars, for instance, to fund research on embryonic and adult stem cells and genomics at universities from Harvard to UCLA."

Bill and Melinda Gates have a similar philosophy with their foundation. Instead of giving away its money piecemeal to the seemingly unlimited number of needy organizations, the Bill and Melinda Gates Foundation picks its projects carefully, looking for where its dollars can make the most demonstrable difference. As the organization states in one of its fifteen core principles: "We take risks, make big bets, and move with urgency. We are in it for the long haul." The results have been astonishing. Through just one of their investments, in the Global Alliance for Vaccines and Immunizations, the foundation is credited with saving more than three million lives.

In 2003, to mark her sixtieth birthday and the beginning of the "give-back" stage of life, Dana Dakin traveled to Ghana, West Africa. After thirty-five years as an entrepreneur in the investments field, Dana was looking for a way to use her skills and her passion to help others. She decided that creating a micro-lending organization in Ghana was the best way to do this. She called her new organization WomensTrust Inc. By providing access to capital directly to poor women, Dana could help them improve their own economic well-being as well as that of their families.

Dana's motto: "Learn, earn, and return—*Globally*."

This is a great way to "give forward," particularly when you can see the change happen. WomensTrust is a conduit between the resources and the needs of the developing world. It is moving from village to village in Africa, so far helping more than 1,000 women who are increasing their incomes with its loans. WomensTrust is giving in other ways, too. The group has provided educational resources to more than 250 women and girls. Nearly 800 women and children have received much-needed medicine from the group to improve their health care.

We may not all be able to give at the levels of the biggest philanthropists of our time, but we can learn from their lessons as we seek to change the world through our own philanthropy, regardless of size.

Another way I've discovered to "provide foreign aid" to help change the world is through a micro-lending organization called Kiva. I was introduced to Kiva through a gift certificate from a friend. For as little as $25 one can invest (by making loans) in small companies in many underdeveloped countries. Returns from an original investment come back on a monthly basis. I keep reinvesting mine. It is amazing to me how much even $25 can help a woman in a small village in Africa to create a business for herself and grow it to include many other women. This is a great way to change the world a few dollars at a time.

With any gift, it's acceptable to think about what results you want from your donation. In my case, one of my donations was to build a scholarship fund. I wanted to do this because I wanted to make difference to a young woman by giving her access to a four-year scholarship. It was a way of making the world a better place for each of my scholarship winners, her parents, family, and community, as well as a way to enhance my legacy, inspiring women and girls to reach their full potential.

Here are some things to ponder while you're considering how to change the world through philanthropy:

- Do you have a plan for your giving?
- Are you giving to a few select recipients you are passionate about and giving where it can do the most good, or are your donations being spread piecemeal across many organizations?
- Is your gift going to make a difference? What is the outcome of your donation?
- How, if at all, would you like to be recognized for your giving?

Philanthropy includes more than just money. You can give your time or your skills just as easily as your dollars. The results can be just as rewarding.

Photographer Nancy Richards Farese found a way to give back to the world through the lens of a camera. The mother of five had been involved in the philanthropic community for most of her life, and got interested in photography about 15 years ago. Then she put the two together to start PhotoPhilanthropy, a San Francisco organization whose mission is to connect photographers with non-profit organizations around the world to tell stories that result in social change. The group's mantra: Change the world with your camera. One of its recent projects was in Haiti, where PhotoPhilanthropy documented the problems surrounding the delivery of aid in the wake of Haiti's horrible earthquake. Another PhotoPhilanthropy project captured the work of non-government organizations trying to rebuild the country of Liberia in the wake of its long civil wars. Here's something else notable about PhotoPhilanthropy: Its leadership team is comprised completely of women.

Greg Mortenson detailed his unique philanthropic activities in the best-selling *Three Cups of Tea* (Viking Penguin, 2006). Mortenson is a mountain climber who in 1993 nearly died trying to climb K2, the world's second-highest peak. He was saved by the people of Korphe, a small village in the remote mountains of Pakistan. To try to repay his rescuers, Mortenson promised to build a school for the village. With Silicon Valley entrepreneur Jean Hoerni, he would go on to start the Central Asia Institute, whose mission is to promote and provide community-based education and literacy programs for girls in Pakistan and Afghanistan.

One of the Central Asia Institute's primary programs is "Pennies for Peace." The idea is that while a penny is almost worthless in places like the United States, it can buy a lot, like pencils, paper, and books, in places like Afghanistan and Pakistan. School students from around the globe have donated more than thirty million pennies to the cause. Additionally, a portion of every book sold also goes to the schools.

Mortenson has said he focuses on girls' education for several reasons. Girls are second-class citizens in the mainly Muslim, Taliban-led regions of Pakistan and Afghanistan. If they do not receive an education from outsiders, they probably will not get an education at all. And since the male-led powers have no incentive to change society and community, the only way it will change is if women and girls are the change agents. Additionally, educating girls makes the most difference in other ways. Giving a girl a mere fifth-grade education can substantially reduce infant mortality rates and improve quality of life in an entire community, according to Mortenson.

He often recites an African proverb when talking about his philanthropic efforts: "If you educate a boy, you educate an individual. If you educate a girl, you educate a community."

Focused giving. Foreign aid. Pennies for Peace.

These are just a few ways to change the world, one small investment at a time. It all makes a difference.

Now It's
Your Turn

12

Dream Big, Change Lives, Change the World

THIS IS AN EXTRAORDINARY TIME to make this world a better place for our having been here, for turning our dreams and big ideas into reality. If you could do one thing to make an impact on women in your family, community, state, nation, or the world, what would it be?

What are the possibilities for helping women and girls in your community? Think big. Remember the message from a previous chapter: "To whom much is given, much is required."

Let's focus on how you bring your "big idea" into reality. Here are some stories of women you may—or may someday—know to get you thinking:

MADAM PRESIDENT?

Hillary Clinton's campaign for president of the United States gave many young women courage to dream big. Among them was ten-year-old Gigi Farley of Tucson. Hopefully we don't need to wait until 2036 for our first woman president of the United States, but Gigi is one eager student.

"In 2036, I'll be eligible to run for president—that is, for president of the United States," says Gigi. A lot of kids grow up dreaming of being president, of course. But Gigi already has a campaign manager, and she is taking lessons from her father, Arizona State Representative Steve Farley. Gigi went door-to-door with her dad on his last campaign.

Gigi wrote an essay in response to The White House Project request to find "She's Out There! 35 Women Under 35 Who Aspire to Lead." She was selected as one of those 35.

Not too long from now, Gigi will want you to vote for her for president. And she says she doesn't have any time to waste. She has to get her experience, beginning now. Gigi has it all figured out. First it will be the student council, then college, law school, city council, state legislature, then governor or a seat in the U.S. Senate.

What got her started? She says her political inspirations came after she stood up to a school bully, determined to defend herself and other girls as well.

"I believe that it is important for leaders to stand up for what is right," she says.

FIRST ON THE BENCH

There was another young lady, a bit older than Gigi, who also had big dreams. She had just graduated from law school and learned about sexual discrimination. Sandra Day O'Connor discovered that the law firms wouldn't hire her except as a secretary. She didn't give up, however, and thank goodness she persevered.

As the first woman on the U.S. Supreme Court, where she built consensus for issues and often was the swing vote, she is widely known for her support for reproductive rights and the death penalty. But long before she paved the way for women on the Supreme Court, O'Connor was working for the advancement of women.

Though she's known more for her career as a jurist, O'Connor in her earlier life was a politician. In 1969, she was appointed to the

Arizona Senate and reelected to two two-year terms, including one in which she served as majority leader of the state senate. A Republican, she fought hard for women's rights while in office. In her 2005 biography about O'Connor, author Joan Biskupic details how Senator O'Connor fought for equal pay and more opportunities in the workplace for women.

Tellingly enough, then-Senator O'Connor also did her own counting of women to show the inequality that existed on the bench, long before she would break the glass ceiling to the most important court in the land. This from Biskupic's book: "'Of the nation's entire roster of 8,750 judges, 300 are women,' (O'Connor) took to saying when she was in the state senate. 'Eight are judges of federal courts.'"

Shortly after she was sworn in as the first woman on the Supreme Court in 1981, O'Connor gave an interview to *Ladies' Home Journal* in which she poignantly summed up her achievement.

"Yes, I will bring the understanding of a woman to the Court, but I doubt that that alone will affect my decisions," she said. "I think the important fact about my appointment is not that I will decide cases as a woman, but that I am a woman who will get to decide cases."

O'Connor's message to other women: Dream Big. Do something out of your comfort zone. Stretch yourself. And then realize that dreams do come true.

FIRST AT THE HELM

U.S. Air Force Colonel Eileen Collins was another "first." She was the first woman selected as a space shuttle pilot, and in 1999, she became the first woman commander of a space shuttle.

Collins' out-of-this-world experience teaches us that anything is possible if you dream big, never quit, and reach for the stars, figuratively and literally.

Collins grew up in Elmira, New York, and she worked hard for everything she got. "She's very thoughtful—nobody ever handed her anything," her parents Jim and Rose Collins said in an interview on a NASA Web site. "Everything she is today, she's earned."

After graduating from high school in 1974, Collins didn't go directly to a university; she went to community college. (Let that be a lesson to anyone who might not be able to attend a big university right out of high school.) She earned an associate degree in mathematics and science from Corning Community College. Along the way, she saved every penny she could until she finally had enough to earn a pilot's license.

Collins' hard work and good grades in community college got her into Syracuse University, where she graduated in 1978. Her grades, her unique flight experience, and her recommendations from professors were enough to earn her a way into the Air Force's pilot training program, making her the first woman to go directly from college to the program.

In the Air Force, she flew C-141 cargo planes and met her soon-to-be husband, Pat. She also began dreaming about going faster, higher, and farther. She set her goals to become an astronaut. In 1986, she earned a master's degree in operations research from Stanford University. Three years later, the community college product earned another master's degree, this one in space systems management from Webster University. She was selected for the astronaut program while attending the Air Force test pilot school, from which she graduated in 1990.

In 1998, at a White House ceremony announcing her as the world's first woman space shuttle commander, Collins explained her big dreams—and challenged others to dream big, too.

"When I was a child, I dreamed about space—I admired pilots, astronauts, and I've admired explorers of all kinds," she said. "It was only a dream that I would someday be one of them. It is my hope that all children—boys and girls—will see this mission and be inspired to reach for their dreams, because dreams do come true!"

FIRST OF HER KIND

Mae Jemison was another girl who grew up looking at the stars, thinking about going into space.

She, too, came from humble beginnings. Her father was a maintenance supervisor for a charity group, and her mother was an elementary school teacher. The family moved from Jemison's native Decatur, Alabama, to Chicago when she was three, because her parents wanted better educational opportunities for their daughter.

During high school, Jemison became interested in engineering. At Stanford University, she majored in chemical engineering and African- and Afro-American Studies, as well as dance and art. If that wasn't enough, she went off to medical school, graduating from Cornell University.

Jemison never abandoned her dreams of going into space, but she also never let her dreams get in the way of other accomplishments, either. As a result, she earned a diverse and unique mix of experience that helped her become an astronaut.

With her medical degree fresh in hand, Jemison worked as a doctor in Los Angeles. Later, she spent two years in the Peace Corps, as a medical officer in Sierra Leone and Liberia, in West Africa. When she returned from her Peace Corps stint, she resumed her medical practice in Los Angeles, all the way working toward her goal of becoming an astronaut. In 1987, she was accepted into the NASA program.

In 1992, she took her medical, chemical engineering, and science training into space, blasting off aboard the space shuttle *Endeavor* as a science mission specialist. During the flight, she conducted experiments in life and material sciences and was a co-investigator in a NASA bone cell research experiment.

Ever since returning to Earth, Jemison has worked to improve the reach of science and technology. She started her own company, the Jemison Group, that researches and markets science for everyday life. Among the company's projects is a satellite-based health care telecommunications network in West Africa. She also started an international science camp for kids aged 12-16.

And you may have seen Jemison yourself. She also hosted a science program on the Discovery Channel, and in 1993 she appeared on an episode of "Star Trek," breaking another barrier by becoming the first real astronaut to ever appear on the television show.

YOUR TURN TO CHANGE THE WORLD

So it's now time for all of us to choose how we want to change the world.

We are all busy. We all face obstacles. But obstacles don't keep a ten-year-old from plotting a way to the White House, keep a community college student from becoming an astronaut, or keep a lawyer from working through sexist comments and discrimination to become a Supreme Court judge.

Busy women get things done. As singer-social activist Bernice Johnson Reagon says, "Life's challenges are not supposed to paralyze you; they're supposed to help you discover who you are."

What are you choosing to be busy doing? What have you discovered about yourself from the challenges you've had?

A Chinese proverb reminds us, "To get through the hardest journey we need take only one step at a time, but we must keep stepping."

There are many steps along the way for you to fulfill your dreams to change the world. So which steps do you take first? In the success stories I've heard and have related to you, the four steps of the methodology to make change happen in my first book, *Become the CEO of You, Inc.*, seem to be same steps that many have used. They are:

1. Create a clear vision.
2. Build a team.
3. Develop a detailed plan.
4. Navigate the journey.

Let's see how they have been used to bring about the change stories we have read about:

Create Your Vision

How would you envision the future after you changed the world, your community, your family, or your work? How would you describe it to others? Begin with the end in mind. Take these steps to help show the way:

1. Identify the problem you are trying to solve.
2. Describe what the future would be like with the problem solved.
3. Develop an "I can do this" mentality.

If you remember the Teacher Home Visit Program, Karen Kalish's "vision" is to get more parents/guardians involved in their children's education. Karen's program specifically would get the parents/guardians into the school, involved in helping their children to be workplace ready or college ready after they graduate from high school. Ultimately, her vision would level the playing field for inner-city children. Once she defined the problem and the outcomes she wanted to achieve, she was ready to fix the problem.

At the Young Women's Leadership Charter School, Joan Hall's dream was to provide an all-girls school experience in the inner city of Chicago and prepare the girls for college and as leaders in their community. She visited a similar school in Harlem that was achieving a similar dream for young girls. After the trip, Joan had confirmed that she had the right vision.

Remember Campus Mentors for Kids? Heidi Schmidt and Kristin Huang, college students from Indiana University, did a needs analysis study and found that inner city kids in grades 1-6 weren't getting the attention they needed to encourage them to go to college. Their vision: to change these kids' worlds. They also knew that college students had high energy and the ability to ignite excitement. Their idea linked the kids and college students together and got the kids excited about continuing their education.

Build Your Team

At this point, it is important you realize that in most cases, implementing change requires more than one person. Where will you find friends and allies to help you create the change you want to implement? After you completed Step 1, you hopefully have started to talk to lots of people about your dream. The more you talk, the more you become committed to bringing your dream to life. You also will find people who want to help you and others who will open doors to people who will help you.

Here are some steps to take:

1. Develop a team of allies who will listen to you and provide honest feedback.

2. Identify members of your project team, those people who will help implement the change.

After visiting the school in Harlem and meeting Ann Tisch, one of its founders, Joan Hall, was ready to take this step for her Young Women Leaders Charter School. She and twenty-two other like-minded, passionate women worked together for two years before the school doors opened.

Develop a Detailed Plan

The lessons from people making a difference are certainly varied, depending on what they were trying to do and for whom. Some would say, "You have the big idea, your allies are with you, and now, just do it." Not so fast. You do have the big idea and your team, but how are you going to get from where you are today to delivering on your promise? This is the phase where you need to create a plan to achieve your vision.

The steps in this phase include:

1. Develop a plan that includes all of the sequential tasks to achieve your vision.
2. Identify the team members who will help you deliver on your promise.
3. Set task assignments and interim goals to ensure you are making progress.

In Philadelphia, the Accenture Women's Network's idea to help inner-city girls become entrepreneurs developed this way. Junior Achievement already had a program to help girls become entrepreneurs. The Accenture women simply identified JA as a great team member. Then all they had to do was create a plan, set task assignments and goals, and monitor the plan to make sure it worked.

Think back to Astronauts Collins and Jemison. At any point along the path to their dream, they certainly could have quit. Becoming a NASA astronaut takes years of hard work, sacrifice, and commitment. It's tough. Yet the two women did it, through years of education, training, and hard work, even if it meant putting off other things or changing their lifestyles to fit in their goals.

Navigate the Journey

This is the phase in which you are actually doing the work necessary to make change happen. The following steps should be considered:

1. Take actions necessary to deliver results.
2. Monitor the progress you are making.
3. Recognize roadblocks; make adjustments when necessary.
4. Celebrate the accomplishment of the change.

Amy Loftus and the other advisors were very excited at the end of the eight-month Junior Achievement Company Program for Girls—and so were the young girls. At the final meeting, they were all beaming with pride in what they had accomplished. This program was life-changing for the fourteen girls, having had experiences that would last them for a lifetime. And based on other successful programs, these girls will be talking about "their company" for years, not only what they learned, but what fun they had creating and operating the business.

So where do you go from here? How will you change the world? What issue will you tackle? Something in education, women's rights, investing in women and girls in your community, taking on a special cause, or making your community a better place to live?

As Betty Friedan said in *The Feminine Mystique*, "We need to liberate ourselves."

I say, "We need to transform ourselves into what we want to be and implement the change we want to see around us."

13
Change Our World, One Woman At A Time

By NOW, WE'VE ESTABLISHED that women have come a long way and that we're still making headway in the world. We've also established that to really change the world and keep moving from simply being "women who are counted" to being "women who count," we must all continue to change our lives, our organizations, our communities, as well as change the way we give our time and our money to others.

There's one other way that women can change the world: Through mentoring. Every woman should have a mentor, and every woman should be a mentor.

Simply put, mentoring makes a difference. Countless studies have shown that mentoring programs help kids stay in schools, help entrepreneurs start successful businesses, help politicians get elected, and help managers and rank-and-file employees alike to climb the leadership ladders at their organizations. As I mentioned in my first book, to get ahead in anything, you need to have a team of people to support you, and one of the members needs to be your mentor.

The U.S. Small Business Administration is a big supporter of mentoring, with programs such as the Women's Network for

Entrepreneurial Training (WNET) and the Office of Women's Business Ownership. The International Mentoring Association creates and promotes best practices for men and women alike. Even with their command-and-control foundation, the armed services emphasize mentoring, too: A U.S. Air Force directive states that, "Mentoring is a fundamental responsibility of all Air Force supervisors."

Mentors have long been an important part of society. The word has its roots in Greek mythology. The first known mention of it was in Homer's *The Odyssey*. When Odysseus left for the Trojan War, according to Homer, he placed his trusted friend Mentor in charge of his palace and of his son, Telemachus. Mentor was asked to be a father figure to young Telemachus while Odysseus was away, and was tasked with advising him, teaching him, challenging him, and encouraging him. In the late 1600s, the French author François Fénelon wrote something of a sequel to Homer's Odyssey that he called *Les Aventures de Télémaque*. Fénelon takes the character Mentor a step further and portrays him as a her—as a woman. In the novel, Mentor is actually revealed to be Minerva, the goddess of wisdom.

An old Chinese proverb also speaks to the value of mentoring. It goes like this:

"If you want one year of prosperity, grow grain; if you want ten years of prosperity, grow trees; if you want one-hundred years of prosperity, grow people."

Growing people is very exciting. I remember how good I would feel every time I reviewed the new partner lists at Accenture and saw someone whom I helped in their career. When I helped someone get a job, it was heartwarming. When I made a suggestion and it helped someone achieve their goals, it encouraged both them and me to do more.

Here's another reason to mentor women: It gets lonely in many positions, especially if you are the only woman or one of only a few women in an organization. I have experienced this firsthand. It is important to have someone to talk to, to share your ideas and frustrations, to build you up when you are down, and to just be a good listener.

First Lady Michelle Obama, when kicking off a girls' mentoring program at the White House in 2009, told of her own experience with mentors.

"Mentoring was the key to my success and being," she said. "There were people who were there for me all along the way. It started with my parents, but there was always a teacher, a neighbor, a coach— somebody in my life that took an extra sort of interest and helped to tell me that I could do it."

Mentoring goes both ways. We must not only *have* mentors, but we must *be* mentors. Through my research, I talk to a lot of women about women. The number one message I hear: "Our role, outside of doing our job and focusing on our own career, is to mentor other women, to help them achieve their goals and aspirations."

Recently I had a conversation with a friend of mine about how to get more women in senior-level positions in corporate America. My friend commented that CEOs are usually so focused on running a business that they don't have time to focus on promoting women. I replied that if they're really concerned with running their business, they ought to make sure they have the best team to help them develop the best solutions to emerging problems, outperform their peers, and appeal to their customer base. These should be diverse teams, I said, including 30-40 percent women if the company wants to deliver more value to their stakeholders and appeal to a broad base of customers, potential customers, and potential employees.

A CEO I once worked for was constantly counting women on teams he was creating. If women were not represented, he would say, "Where are the women, and what is the progression plan to have them at the table?" That's the only way that change is going to happen in our companies, our organizations, and our world. We must have teams with varied intellectual powers, harnessing both genders' thoughts and experiences. Both women and men in senior-level positions need to make sure this is happening all around us.

There are two approaches to mentoring: Formal mentoring and informal mentoring. In the more formal relationship, the mentee should be responsible for the relationship, for setting meetings, and for setting the direction of discussions. At the beginning of a relationship, goals and objectives should be clearly set, and meetings should be held specifically to try to discover ways to meet those goals and objectives. In an informal mentoring arrangement, the conversations are ad hoc. Perhaps something just happened at work or in your family and you just need to talk. Even so, the mentee should have a goal in mind for the meeting, such as to discuss an issue on their mind, gain insight, or find a new way to move forward.

Whether formally or informally, mentors need to help their mentees find the right paths to their goals and destinations and the right tasks to get there. A good mentor can provide on-the-job training and is an independent source of help and support in a non-threatening environment.

Not sure how a mentor might help you? I've included some great mentoring advice at the end of this chapter from other women.

If your organization has a formal mentoring program, take advantage of the opportunity. If it doesn't, find a mentor through your own channels—maybe someone who has the job you would like to prepare yourself for, a role model, or a woman who you admire, trust, and whose advice you value.

My message: If you don't have a mentor, find one.

I have always been fortunate to have good mentors throughout my life, from my parents to my high school math teacher to my former bosses and co-workers. One of the most important messages I heard from one of my mentors, a very well-respected partner at Arthur Andersen & Co., was a simple sign of encouragement. "Susan, you *can* be a partner," he told me. This was the first time anybody ever said that to me. He helped me to think big and to begin to make things happen. In another situation, an advocate of mine told the partner I was working with that he wanted me in the partnership and that the partner should provide me with the roles and responsibilities to make that happen. I didn't even know this was going on at the time but, as a result, I did indeed become a partner.

I still have many mentors who help me each and every day. And through my books, my newsletters, and my website, I like to think of myself as a "virtual mentor" to anyone who reads or hears what I have to say.

So now it's your turn. If each of us mentored one woman, imagine how we could change our organizations. Imagine how we could change the world!

TIPS ON MENTORING—AND BEING MENTORED

Think Big, Stay Focused

Erin Slater (Campus Mentors for Kids) reinforces how important it is to think big. "Have an abundance mentality," she says. "For example, whatever you are thinking, think bigger. And have confidence in your big ideas. You can't meet enough people, but focusing on key relationships is important, too. What can you do to build new relationships and enhance the relationships you already have?" As we talked, Erin also told me how important it is to stay focused on whatever you decide to do. Don't change your direction unless your plan changes your priorities. They have merit, so explore them and "make them happen."

Be a Great Listener

One of the most important skills of a mentor is to be a great listener. Patty Robinson of Accenture says that by being a good listener, you can change the life of the person you are listening to and even your own. A good listener is not someone who immediately gets into the problem-solving mode (with a lot of solutions). A good listener asks good questions and is empathetic, which often times helps the mentee come up with their own solutions.

Good Mentoring Opportunities

Many mentors will say that a one-on-one conversation or just an interaction with anyone is potentially a good mentoring opportunity. Virginia Washington of Ford Motor Company told me about an executive who read the *Wall Street Journal* every day. When he was finished with it, he put it on her desk. "What a subtle way to let me know I should read the *Journal* and it left an impression on me," she says.

Irene Rosenfeld, CEO of Kraft Foods Inc., says you should be a good mentor by modeling the behaviors you expect of others. "The behaviors we try to model at Kraft are: We inspire trust, we act like owners, we keep it simple, we're inclusive. I challenge both myself and my management team to live these values and behave accordingly. We can't expect our employees to do it if we don't do it ourselves. And we expect employees to call us on our behaviors if we don't model them."

Ask for Help

Maybe Michelle Obama put it best when she started the White House girls mentoring program: "The biggest thing to remember is that you have to ask for help and be open to getting the help."

We need to understand that we don't always have the answer for every problem that comes our way. We need to test our ideas on others. It is useful and liberating at times to ask for input from others. Lisa Mascolo of Accenture would say it is a way to bring others in "under the tent" with you. After such a discussion, your direction may be clearer or the idea you discussed may be better. And you aren't there by yourself. You have others "under the tent" with you.

Be Present

Michele Roden of BluOpal Consulting uses the phrase: "There is no time like the present." Keeping focus on the here and now allows for a rich and often joyful life experience. Decisions are best made from being in the present moment—not being driven by the past (what has always been done or what has been expected) or by the future (what is supposed to be done) but by what is needed now. When people take the time to check in with what is true in the moment, choices are made with the best and most relevant information. Relationships benefit also, because people feel when others are mentally and emotionally there. Windows of opportunity, large and small, only come in the present moment.

Learn from Disappointment

Several years ago, Jane Prescott-Smith was working on an agreement between her company and a nonprofit organization to market a healthy diet campaign. The company didn't approve the agreement. Jane was furious. Friends suggested that she learn to accept the things she couldn't change. Her productivity slipped, and her boss noticed. He even suggested a lateral move to begin a "fresh start." Jane was determined to be honest to herself—the company had evolved and she hadn't. "We were no longer a good fit," she said.

With newfound clarity, she left her company to plunge into the nonprofit world where she has spent the last two decades, mostly with the University of Arizona. "My lesson: Learn from disappointment. After playing the blame game and realizing I was out of sync with my company, it was clear it was time for me to leave," she says. "Be true to yourself so you can look forward to starting every day."

Find Your Voice

Tricia Emerson of Emerson Human Capital has read a lot of Deborah Tannen's books about finding your voice, such as *You Just Don't Understand* (Ballantine, 1991) and *I Only Say This Because I Love You* (Random House, 2001). Tricia mentions how often she sees women giving away their power because they're afraid to express their own views—because they don't find their own voice.

This can be a way of demeaning yourself. Yes, it's good to be nice and polite. Sometimes it's good to not make waves or be confrontational. But it's another thing to allow others to run your life, derail your dreams, and keep you from accomplishing your goals just because you don't speak up for yourself or make yourself heard.

14
Changes and Shifts

WHEN I WAS GROWING UP, one of my favorite places in the world was the cabin my father built on Lake Bracken, a long, skinny, and beautiful little lake in central Illinois. My family's place wasn't much, but what it lacked in grandeur it made up for in love and fun. My father literally built it with his own hands, starting from two horse stalls that would ultimately become the kitchen and the bathroom. We had many wonderful times there and more laughs than could ever be counted.

As I grew older, I knew I wanted a place like that cabin on Lake Bracken. I finally got it in 2003. Appropriately enough, I opened it with a family reunion, even though it is far from that horse-stall cabin on the little lake in Illinois.

My place on the water is perched on the rim of the Pacific Ocean on the Central Oregon coast. From every room, I have views of the world's biggest ocean and spectacular sunsets that are interrupted only by the occasional sighting of a whale headed south or a storm headed inland.

It, too, is a special place. I wrote my last book here, and I wrote much of this book here also.

Everything is built on sand dunes, of course, and depending on the weather you can sometimes see the land shift and change right in front of your eyes. I am an early riser, and from my second-floor office or my deck I can watch the morning beach walkers make their way down the coast each day, marching toward some unseen goal, their footsteps disappearing in the sand behind them with every wave.

I often find myself thinking about the women's movement as I watch. Day by day, year by year, for so very long, we have gradually changed the landscape around us, just as the waves constantly change the beach before me. Over time, so many women before us have left their mark on this world and shown us a path to the future, if only we choose to follow in their footsteps before they fade away.

I think back to all of the things that had to change just to get us to the place we are today. I think of the wartime women who bound their breasts and disguised themselves as men just so they could fight alongside them; of the women who later stayed home and fed a nation, raised its children, and built its weapons in the factories and shipyards; of those female pioneers in business and industry who slowly but surely paved the way from the secretarial pool to the boardroom and opened so many doors for us all. I think about all the rules that had to be rewritten just so we could have some semblance of equality: How we had to change the law just to get the right to vote, the right to equal pay, and the right to equal opportunities in academics and sports.

And yet I am reminded that we still have a Declaration of Independence that declares that all *men* are created equal, a workplace where women still earn two-thirds of what men make, and a world where women and girls in some countries are still denied an education.

Yes, the world has changed.

More women are getting involved in politics today than they have in decades. People are starting to realize the need to do more to fill the educational pipelines with bright young women in the science, technology, engineering, and mathematics (STEM) fields if the United States is going to continue as a leader in innovation. The young women in those pipelines will be tomorrow's inventors, scientists, and Nobel laureates. They will be the creators—the leaders—of the twenty-first century. Without them, we cannot remain the greatest country in the world.

Of course, the workplace is changing too. The opportunities for women in business and industry are greater than ever before. The fact that about half of all workers in America today are women is a testament to how far we've come from the days when females were considered inadequate workers whose place was in the home, not the office or job site. Companies are indeed at least considering diversity and promoting more women to top management, and female CEOs are no longer unheard of (even though it has taken us more than a century to get here).

But we still have so much more to change.

We must continue to work to put the status of women on a firmer footing, one built not on sand that can change and shift under pressure, but one built on rock that is solid.

As I was putting together this last chapter, I talked to a friend of mine at Accenture. She was so excited, because she was working on a company-wide program to mark International Women's Day (March 8th) at my former firm. For several years, the firm has made a big deal about International Women's Day. It is now celebrated in approximately one hundred of Accenture's offices around the world. This is truly a celebration of how far women have come, designed to energize them and to give them an opportunity to network with other successful women. I applaud the firm for what they are doing for women.

I couldn't help but think back to my days as the first woman partner at the firm, back when I was an "Andersen man in a skirt," and how unheard of something like this would've been back then. How far the company—and women—had come. In the early days, at partner meetings, we women would have breakfast together at a table in a huge room full of men. At first there were only two or three of us. We really celebrated when we had a full table.

Kathleen Matthews has seen both sides of the quandary. As the executive vice president of global communications and public affairs for Marriott International Inc., she is partly responsible for promoting diversity and equal opportunity programs within the hotel chain. In her previous career as a Washington, D.C. television news reporter and anchor for thirty years, she experienced what it was like being a rarity in her profession. (She also reported extensively on it as the host of a syndicated television magazine show called "Working Woman" that aired in seventy-five markets nationwide.)

At a 2009 women's conference in Washington, Matthews explained how she would measure the success of women.

"I'm always counting (people) whenever I walk into a room," she told attendees at the Bisnow media conference on the status of women in work and society. "At the (television) station, I was the one woman, and there were three white guys and one black guy. When we get to the point where we're not counting anymore, that's when I think we'll have reached success."

I do the same thing at every committee meeting, every organizational announcement, every business event I attend. The numbers are changing, but we still have a long way to go. When I can walk into a room and at least 30 percent of the participants are women, I will say we've reached success.

To be sure, we're doing a lot less counting these days. Though the numbers are still small, it's no longer a surprise to see a woman at the television anchor desk or running her own business. Women's issues also are more intertwined in the most important policy issues of the day, from health care reform to economic recovery. And once again, it seems that women are essential to helping fix some of the world's problems, be they international relations, homeland security, or the collapse of the global economy—all problems that I believe are connected to the fact that our governments, our economies, and our societies have been dominated by men for so long.

The question is, will our new movement be a temporary movement, like it was for all the "Rosie the Riveters" and "farmerettes" from World War I and II, when women came out in force but then faded back into their traditional places in society? Or will it be something more sustained and permanent, like the days following Betty Friedan's *The Feminine Mystique* in the 1960s, when women began to accomplish so many new "firsts"?

When I hear the stories and talk to people like Karen Kalish and Erin Slater and Gigi Farley, the ten-year-old who is already plotting her way to the presidency with the help of organizations like the White House Project, I can't help but think we are in an age more like the latter. If we are not at a tipping point, we are at least at a turning point, much like in the 1960s when the attitudes toward women would change forever.

Women and girls like Karen, Erin, Gigi, and countless others are inspiring to me because they're taking the next step. They're going beyond thinking about problems and talking about problems and actually doing something about them.

Yes, we still have glass ceilings to break and boardrooms to enter. Yes, we still need equality in pay. But the headway and the accomplishments we made in the past have created a new world for all of us today, a new world filled with opportunities for us to shape and change the world even more for the women who will follow us in the future.

My friend Susan Neely, CEO of the American Beverage Association, had some great advice in an essay she wrote recently. She called it "Becoming a Catalyst for Change—Perspectives of a Female CEO." Susan's personal experiences moving up the career ladder, which aren't a lot different from mine, are reflective of women in general over the years. They could also serve as good lessons as we move from the phase of "counting women" to becoming "women who count."

"For the first part of my career, I looked for ways to make change within the current system," she wrote. "The strategy was to get in the door. Get promoted. Amass power and then provoke change. In more recent years, I've found there are times when it is both necessary and effective to be direct in provoking change.

"Change can start through women leaders (who) have the courage to do things differently," Susan wrote. "Why perpetuate the same foolish system . . . don't be afraid to be a different kind of leader."

Just like Susan, and just like so many other female pioneers who broke the barriers of sexism to become astronauts, politicians, Supreme Court judges, and so much more, we must all have the courage to be a "different kind of leader," so we don't "perpetuate the same foolish system" that is at least partly to blame for many of the problems we have in the world today. We need to do this not just for women's sake, but for society's sake. More women in leadership roles means new ways of approaching old problems, whether it's how we deal with climate change or international relations or the responsibilities of business and government.

What are *you* going to do to change the system? What are you going to do to change the world? You've already invested your time and your money in this book, so how can you leverage that investment next?

As a life coach and mentor, I challenge my mentees to push themselves to new levels, not just for themselves, but for everyone they work with, live with, and associate with. In essence, I push them to change themselves so they can change the world.

I want to challenge you similarly. Ask yourself this question: What is the change I want to affect in the world over the next three to five years?

Don't just think about this in passing and forget it. And don't limit yourself. Think big. Write your answer down. Bring it to life, at least on paper. Then remember the steps I described earlier:

- Begin with the end in mind. Describe what the end result would look like if you're successful.
- Gather your team. Talk about this with your friends, your colleagues, your family. Incorporate their suggestions and let them help you.
- Develop your goals and create your plan. Don't wait for something to happen *to* you; make it happen *for* you.
- Find a mentor, a "nudger," a coach, to push you to make your change happen, to encourage you, to help you over the hurdles that will certainly come.

And then make it happen.

It won't be easy, and it won't be simple, and it won't always be clear.

But remember that as long as we dream big, beginning with the end in mind; take our teams along with us, mentoring others along the way; make and follow our plans; and navigate our way to a successful outcome, every one of us will be a woman who made a difference. We will be women who count.

And together, we will change the world.

[A GUIDE TO FURTHER READING]

Books

America's Women, Gail Collins (HarperCollins, 2003)

Become the CEO of You, Inc., Susan Bulkeley Butler (Purdue University Press, 2006)

Faces of Feminism, Sheila Tobias (Westview Press, 1997)

Fruits of Victory, Elaine F. Weiss (Potomac Books, 2008)

Half the Sky: Turning Oppression into Opportunity for Women Worldwide, Nicholas D. Kristof and Sheryl WuDunn (Random House, 2009)

I Only Say This Because I Love You, Deborah Tannen (Random House, 2001)

Mobilizing Woman-Power, Harriot Stanton Blatch (The Woman's Press, 1918)

No Turning Back: The History of Feminism and the Future of Women, Estelle B. Freedman (Ballantine Books, 2002)

Notes from the Cracked Ceiling, Anne E. Kornblut (Crown, 2009)

Now, Discover Your Strengths, Marcus Buckingham and Donald O. Clifton (Free Press, 2001)

Rumors of Our Progress Have Been Greatly Exaggerated, Carolyn B. Maloney (Rodale, 2008)

Stones into Schools, Greg Mortenson (Viking, 2009)

The Feminine Mystique, Betty Friedan (Norton, 1963)

The Managerial Woman, Margaret Hennig and Anne Jardim (Anchor Press/Doubleday, 1977)

Three Cups of Tea, Greg Mortenson (Viking Penguin, 2006)

Why Women Should Rule the World, Dee Dee Myers (HarperCollins, 2008)

What Happy Working Mothers Know, Cathy L. Greenberg and Barrett S. Avigdor (Wiley, 2009)

What Happy Women Know, Dan Baker and Cathy L. Greenberg (Rodale, 2007)

When Everything Changed: The Amazing Journey of American Women from 1960 to the Present, Gail Collins (Little, Brown, 2009)

Womenomics, Claire Shipman and Katty Kay (HarperCollins, 2009)

You Just Don't Understand: Women and Men in Conversation, Deborah Tannen (Ballantine, 1991)

Reports

The White House Project Report: Benchmarking Women's Leadership, The White House Project, November 2009

The Shriver Report: A Woman's Nation Changes Everything, Maria Shriver and the Center for American Progress, October 2009

[ACKNOWLEDGMENTS]

It has been nearly five decades since I graduated from Purdue University and entered the business world. *The Feminine Mystique* was the guidebook for women of that era. Now, after a fulfilling and successful career, I have my own book that I hope will serve as something of a guide for women of this era.

In this new decade, which I envision as the "Decade for Women," I have a message to all women: It's time to change our world. More than 50 percent of the nation's population is comprised of women, as is around 50 percent of its workforce and more than 50 percent of its college graduates. Yet only a small percentage of our country's elected and appointed leaders are women. We deserve equality. We deserve to be in the discussions where all the important decisions are being made that affect our lives. There is no time like the present to make this happen, to move from "counting women" to "women who count," and to ensure that all men and women are equal.

So many people have helped me to realize that I am now a twenty-first century feminist, with the passion to understand that it is time to be (and to create) the change that we want to see in the world, as Mahatma Gandhi taught us. Thank you for getting me to this new space.

To my longtime friend and "chief nudger" Harvard MBA Karen Page, who helped me envision not only this book and what it could mean to future generations of women (and men) around the world, but also helped me envision my previous book and my institute. She is always available when I need a helping hand. Karen is a very important member of my "team," who provides me with the advice and counsel that I need when I have a new idea, like changing the world. Karen, thank you for everything you have done to help me be where I am today, changing the world.

To all of my advocates and mentors who have always encouraged me to "think big," to create the future and then make it happen, thank you for getting me to the space where I am today.

There are so many who have physically made this book a reality, including the people at Purdue University Press, who were willing to take my first book, *Become the CEO of You, Inc.*, after my first publisher closed its doors. To Charles Watkinson and Bryan Shaffer who were willing to do something a little different for an academic publishing house, I give special thanks.

Then of course a thank you to all who agreed to be interviewed for my book: Barrett Avigdor, Audrey Goins Brichi, Cathy Bruni, Kathy Calvin, La Shenna Clark, Ahne Titus, France Córdova, Joann DiGennaro, Laura Edlin, Tricia Emerson, Ursie Fairbairn, Gigi Farley, Anne Gardner, Reedi Garrett, Joan Hall, Lisa Johnson, Pam Krahl, Karen Kalish, Tamara Keefe, Amanda Koushyar, Zara Larsen, Amy Loftus, Lisa Mascolo, Jane Eyre McDonald, Marisa Murray, Susan Neely, Carla Paonessa, Laura Penny, Lisa Reither, Joyce Richards, Patty Robinson, Michele Roden, Erin Slater, Jane Prescott Smith, Sue Sonnichsen, Vanessa Truett, Virginia Washington, and Mary Ann Zimmerman. Without you I couldn't have gleaned the information about how women already are changing the world. I want to make sure that each of my readers is able to find themselves in my book, with a passion to make real change wherever they are in life. I hope you will make change happen, so thank you. And to Susan Krieger, who provided such encouragement and positive feedback after reading my book, thank you.

Thanks also to Michele Roden, my P.E.O. sister, a coach, and a good friend who led me to Bob Keefe. Without him, this book wouldn't have been completed. It has been a fun journey, and I offer him my sincere thanks for helping me change the world.

Thank goodness for my home in Oregon, which I have found is the best place to write. Both of my books have been "birthed" there. What a wonderful place to sit and watch the ocean and to be in the right mind to let my thoughts flow

And of course there is my immediate and extended family across the country and around the globe. You were always there for me, supporting and encouraging me.

And thank you to my parents, who have been watching and guiding me from afar, continuing to let me know that I can do anything I set my mind to. With this book I certainly have taken another big step, this time to change the world.

Finally, to my spiritual leader, who is always there as my "co-pilot," who is with me all the time and guides my life, thank you.

Susan Bulkeley Butler
September 2010